## Table of Contents

| | | |
|---|---|---|
| Unit 1 | Vowel short /**a**/ | 3 |
| Unit 2 | Vowel short /**e**/ | 9 |
| Unit 3 | Vowel short /**i**/ | 15 |
| Unit 4 | Vowel short /**o**/ | 21 |
| Unit 5 | Vowel short/**u**/ | 27 |
| Unit 6 | Review tests | 201-208 |
| | | |
| Unit 7 | Vowel long /**a**/ | 34 |
| Unit 8 | Vowel long /**e**/ | 40 |
| Unit 9 | Vowel long /**i**/ | 46 |
| Unit 10 | Vowel long /**o**/ | 52 |
| Unit 11 | Phonograms **ow, old** | 58 |
| Unit 12 | Review tests | 209-216 |
| | | |
| Unit 13 | Phonograms **ow, ew** | 65 |
| Unit 14 | Phonograms **ay, ake** | 71 |
| Unit 15 | Phonograms **ing, ill** | 77 |
| Unit 16 | Phonograms **and, ent** | 83 |
| Unit 17 | Phonograms **all, ell** | 89 |
| Unit 18 | Review tests | 217-224 |
| | | |
| Unit 19 | Consonant clusters **sl, pl** | 96 |
| Unit 20 | Consonant clusters **br, tr** | 102 |
| Unit 21 | Consonant clusters **gr, fr** | 108 |
| Unit 22 | Consonant digraph **sh,** | 114 |
| Unit 23 | Consonant digraph **th,** | 120 |
| Unit 24 | Review tests | 225-232 |
| | | |
| Unit 25 | Suffix **ing** | 127 |
| Unit 26 | Plural nouns with **s** | 133 |
| Unit 27 | Suffix **s** with verbs | 139 |
| Unit 28 | Suffix **ed** | 145 |
| Unit 29 | Contractions | 151 |
| Unit 30 | Review tests | 233-240 |

Unit 31 Vowel sound /ü/ .................................................................. 158
Unit 32 **R** -controlled vowels /är/, /ôr/ ........................................ 164
Unit 33 Consonant digraphs **sh, th** ............................................. 170
Unit 34 Homophones ..................................................................... 176
Unit 35 Compound words ............................................................... 182
Unit 36 Review tests ................................................................ 241-248

Alphabet chart.................................................................................. 189

Spelling Glossary ..................................................................... 190-200

---

My recommendation is to remove the answer key and unit tests before book is given to the student. Lesson plans are one page per day Monday through Wednesday. Thursday's work is writing the words three times each on pages provided. The test is to be given on Friday. Give the review test for units indicated. It is recommended that one test per day be given for unit tests.

---

### Grace and Glory Curriculum
Written by
Victoria Kays

# Unit 1

1. flat
2. brag
3. drag
4. clap
5. match
6. mash
7. flag
8. fast
9. that
10. slap

These words have the short *a* vowel sound you hear at the beginning of the word *at*.

**A.** Write the spelling words that end with the letters **at**.

1. _____  2. _____

**B.** Write the spelling words that end with the letters **ap**.

1. _____  2. _____

**C.** Write the spelling words that end with the letters **ag**.

1. _____  2. _____

3. _____

**D.** Write the spelling words that begin with the letter **m**.

1. _____  2. _____

**E.** Write the spelling word that ends with the consonant cluster **st**.

_____

**F.** Write the spelling words that begin with the consonant cluster **fl**.

1. _____  2. _____

**A.** Write the spelling word that goes with each meaning.

1. to move something along slowly _____

2. a rectangular piece of cloth that is used to represent a nation

   _____

3. a thing used to start a fire _____

4. to speak too highly of one's self _____

5. to crush _____

**B.** Write these words in **a-b-c** order.

    slap       clap       that       flat       fast

1. _____

2. _____

3. _____

4. _____

5. _____

Write the spelling word that belongs in each sentence.

1. It is not nice to _____ someone in the face.

2. Please _____ the potatoes for me.

3. Our _____ has fifty stars on it.

4. Do not _____ the box across the floor.

5. I do not like to mow grass if the ground is not _____.

6. Some people _____ their hands when they sing.

7. You might fall if you run too _____.

8. We should not _____ on ourselves.

9. You can start a fire with a _____.

10. Do you know _____ teacher?

Write the spelling words three times.

1. flat _____  _____

    _____

2. brag _____  _____

    _____

3. drag _____  _____

    _____

4. clap _____  _____

    _____

5. match _____  _____

    _____

6. mash_____  _____

    _____

7. flag _____ _____

_____

8. fast _____ _____

_____

9. that _____ _____

_____

10. slap_____ _____

_____

# Unit 2

1. shed
2. press
3. less
4. bled
5. left
6. step
7. mess
8. fled
9. crest
10. dwell

These words have the short *e* vowel sound you hear at the beginning of the word ***egg***.

**A.** Write the spelling words that end with the letters **ed.**

1._____  2. _____


3._____

**B.** Write the spelling words that end with the letters **ss.**

1._____  2. _____


3._____

**C.** Write the spelling word that ends with the letters **ll.**


_____

**D.** Write the spelling word that ends with the consonant cluster **ft**.


_____

**E.** Write the spelling word that begins with the consonant cluster **st**.


_____

**F.** Write the spelling word that begins and ends with a consonant cluster.


_____

**A.** Write the spelling word that goes with each meaning.

1. to stay for a while in one place _____

2. a small building for storage _____

3. the opposite of right _____

4. the opposite of more _____

5. the top of a hill _____

**B.** Write these words in **a-b-c** order.

    **press**    **bled**    **step**    **mess**    **fled**

1. _____

2. _____

3. _____

4. _____

5. _____

Write the spelling word that belongs in each sentence.

1. It looked like the people _____ from a dinosaur.

2. _____ down on the paper after you put glue on it.

3. Do not leave a _____ on the table.

4. David said he would _____ in the house of the Lord forever.

5. The wreck happened at the _____ of the hill.

6. Ben eats _____ than I do.

7. Some people use their _____ hand for writing.

8. The boys were to help build the _____.

9. His cut finger _____ a lot.

10. Be careful where you _____ if you go walking in the forest.

12

Write the spelling words three times.

1. shed _____ _____

   _____

2. press _____ _____

   _____

3. less _____ _____

   _____

4. bled _____ _____

   _____

5. left _____ _____

   _____

6. step_____ _____

   _____

7. mess _____ _____

_____

8. fled _____ _____

_____

9. crest _____ _____

_____

10. dwell _____ _____

_____

# Unit 3

1. disk
2. brim
3. chin
4. skim
5. blimp
6. wind
7. thin
8. swim
9. limp
10. friend

These words have the short *i* vowel sound you hear at the beginning of the word *it*.

**A.** Write the spelling words that end with the letters **im**.

1. _____  2. _____

3. _____

**B.** Write the spelling words that end with the letters **in**.

1. _____  2. _____

**C.** Write the spelling words that end with the consonant cluster **mp**.

1. _____  2. _____

**D.** Write the spelling words that end with the consonant cluster **nd**.

1. _____  2. _____

**E.** Write the spelling word that ends with the consonant cluster **sk**.

_____

**F.** Write the spelling word that ends with the word **end**.

_____

**A.** Write the spelling word that goes with each meaning.

1. an airship _____

2. not thick _____

3. to glide along in water _____

4. something round and flat that can be used to store information

   _____

5. to walk with difficulty _____

6. to read quickly over something; low-fat milk

   _____

**B.** Write these words in **a-b-c** order.

    **friend**        **brim**        **wind**        **chin**

1. _____

2. _____

3. _____

4. _____

Use spelling words to complete the sentences.

1. You can see a _____ float across the sky close to the time for the Kentucky Derby.

2. Frankie had lost weight and was very _____.

3. Donna had stitches in her _____ after the wreck.

4. It is dangerous to _____ in the river.

5. A true _____ will want to stay with you till the end.

6. Fat free milk is also called _____ milk.

7. Did she save the pictures on a computer _____?

8. The _____ was blowing hard.

9. I was walking with a _____.

10. Do not fill the cup to the _____.

Write the spelling words three times.

1. disk _____  _____

   _____

2. brim _____  _____

   _____

3. chin _____  _____

   _____

4. skim _____  _____

   _____

5. blimp _____  _____

   _____

6. wind _____  _____

   _____

7. thin _____ _____

   _____

8. swim _____ _____

   _____

9. limp _____ _____

   _____

10. friend _____ _____

    _____

# Unit 4

1. cost
2. blot
3. lost
4. boss
5. shop
6. clot
7. floss
8. spot
9. chop
10. crop

These words have the short *o* vowel sound you hear at the beginning of the word *off*.

**A.** Write the spelling words that end with the letters **ot.**

1._____  2._____

3._____

**B.** Write the spelling words that end with the letters **op.**

1._____  2._____

3._____

**C.** Write the spelling words that end with the letters **ss.**

1._____  2._____

**D.** Write the spelling words that end with the consonant cluster **st.**

1._____  2._____

**E.** Write the spelling words that begin with a consonant digraph.

1._____  2._____

**A.** Unscramble these words and write them correctly.

1. hosp _____

2. tosc _____

3. rpco _____

4. sofls _____

5. tlbo _____

**B.** Write the spelling word that goes with each meaning.

1. to cut into small pieces _____

2. not found _____

3. one who is in control of others _____

4. a small part that is different _____

5. a thick mass of blood _____

Use spelling words to complete the sentences.

1. The teacher is the _____ in the class.

2. I hope we have a good _____ of potatoes.

3. Did you use _____ on your teeth?

4. The key to the van was _____.

5. How much did it _____ to get another key?

6. Earl could _____ the wood after he took it home.

7. There was a white _____ on the carpet where milk was spilled.

8. The woman was in the craft _____.

9. There was a yellow _____ on the shirt.

10. A scab is like a _____ of dried blood.

Write the spelling words three times.

1. cost _____ _____

   _____

2. blot _____ _____

   _____

3. lost _____ _____

   _____

4. boss _____ _____

   _____

5. shop _____ _____

   _____

6. clot _____ _____

   _____

7. floss _____  _____

_____

8. spot _____  _____

_____

9. chop _____  _____

_____

10. crop _____  _____

_____

# Unit 5

1. rust
2. brush
3. club
4. must
5. crush
6. hush
7. dust
8. buck
9. fuss
10. plug

These words have the short *u* vowel sound you hear at the beginning of the word *us*.

**A.** Write the spelling words that end with the consonant cluster **st**.

1. _____   2. _____

3. _____

**B.** Write the spelling words that end with the consonant digraph **sh**.

1. _____   2. _____

3. _____

**C.** Write the spelling word that ends with the letters **ug**.

_____

**D.** Write the spelling word that ends with the letters **ss**.

_____

**E.** Write the spelling word that names each picture.

1. _____

2. _____

A. Write these words in **a-b-c** order.

**hush**     **rust**     **must**     **plug**     **club**

1. _____

2. _____

3. _____

4. _____

5. _____

B. Write the spelling word that goes with each meaning.

1. a male deer _____

2. a thing used to fix hair _____

3. small pieces of dirt _____

4. to press or squeeze _____

5. to complain _____

Write the spelling word that belongs in each sentence.

1. Frankie wanted the women to _____

   so he could go to sleep.

2. He did not like to hear them _____.

3. Maybe he should have tried an ear _____

   in each ear.

4. You can _____ an orange to make

   orange juice.

5. The truck had _____ under the door.

6. Please wipe the _____ off the shelves.

7. Some people like to play golf, so they carry a golf

   _____ with them.

8. Let me _____ my hair before

   we leave.

9. Children _____ obey their parents.

10. Was the deer a doe or a _____?

Write the spelling words three times.

1. rust _____ _____

   _____

2. brush _____ _____

   _____

3. club _____ _____

   _____

4. must _____ _____

   _____

5. crush _____ _____

   _____

6. hush _____ _____

   _____

7. dust _____  _____

   _____

8. buck _____  _____

   _____

9. fuss _____  _____

   _____

10. plug _____  _____

    _____

# Unit 6

# Time for Review tests

Ask your teacher for the tests.

# Unit 7

1. take    2. gave

3. made    4. came

5. name    6. game

7. ate     8. make

9. gate    10. safe

These spelling words have the long **a** sound you hear in *make.* This sound is made by *a* + **consonant** + *e.*

**A.** Write the spelling words that end with the letters **ake.**

1._____ 2. _____

**B.** Write the spelling words that end with the letters **ame.**

1._____ 2. _____

3._____

**C.** Write the spelling words that contain the letters **ate.**

1._____ 2. _____

**D.** Vowels are missing from these words. Fill in the missing vowels.

1. m____d____          2. s____f____

3. g____v____

**E.** Write the spelling words that start with the letter **g.**

1._____ 2. _____

3._____

**A.** One word in each set is not spelled correctly. Write the word correctly.

1. make    made    gaev    _____

2. name    taik    game    _____

3. aet    came    make    _____

4. maed    name    game    _____

**B.** Write these spelling words in **a-b-c** order.

**make    game    came    name    gate    safe**

1. _____  4. _____

2. _____  5. _____

3. _____  6. _____

**C.** Write the spelling word that belongs in each set.

1. make and _____

2. come and _____

Write the spelling word that belongs in each sentence. The first letter is given for you.

1. Can you make a **g**_____?

2. How can you **m**_____ one?

3. What will you **n**_____ your game?

4. **T**_____ time to think of who will play it.

5. Make sure your game is **s**_____ to play.

6. The boys did not bring their game when they **c**_____ to my house.

7. Someone **g**_____ them money to buy something.

8. We **a**_____ breakfast and left to go on a trip.

9. A fun game **m**_____ our trip more enjoyable.

10. Do you think we should name our game "Open the **G**_____ and Let the Monkeys Out?

Write the spelling words three times.

1. take  _____  _____

   _____

2. gave  _____  _____

   _____

3. made  _____  _____

   _____

4. came  _____  _____

   _____

5. name  _____  _____

   _____

6. game  _____  _____

   _____

7. ate _____ _____

_____

8. make _____ _____

_____

9. gate _____ _____

_____

10. safe _____ _____

_____

# Unit 8

1. read
2. seed
3. feed
4. need
5. weed
6. beam
7. keep
8. peep
9. team
10. seam

These words have the long *e* vowel sound you hear in the word *see*. When two vowels are together in a word, the first one usually makes its long sound, and the second one is usually silent.

**A.** Write the spelling words in which the letters **ee** make the long **e** sound.

1. _____  2. _____

3. _____  4. _____

5. _____  6. _____

**B.** Write the spelling words in which the letters **ea** make the long **e** sound.

1. _____  2. _____

3. _____  4. _____

**C.** Write the spelling words that start with the letter **s**.

1. _____  2. _____

**D.** Write the spelling word that starts and ends with the same letter.

_____

**E.** Write the spelling words that name things that can grow in a garden.

1. _____  2. _____

**A.** Unscramble these spelling words and write them correctly.

1. defe _____

2. pkee _____

3. ader _____

4. meta _____

5. meas _____

**B.** Write these words in **a-b-c** order.

      seed        need        weed        beam        peep

1. _____

2. _____

3. _____

4. _____

5. _____

**C.** Write the word that is like the sound a baby chicken makes.

_____

Use spelling words to complete the sentences.

1. Vickie wanted to grow tomatoes from a _____.

2. She did not want one _____ to be with her plant.

3. She decided to _____ in a book to learn what to do.

4. She wanted to grow enough tomatoes to _____ her family.

5. She would _____ some good soil.

6. She would need to tie the plants up to _____ them from falling.

7. A _____ of sunshine would help them grow.

8. She did not want to hear the _____ of little chickens in her garden.

9. She did not want to tear a _____ in her dress while she worked in her garden.

10. Maybe she could grow enough to feed a whole _____.

Write the spelling words three times.

1. read _____ _____

_____

2. seed _____ _____

_____

3. feed _____ _____

_____

4. need _____ _____

_____

5. weed _____ _____

_____

6. beam _____ _____

_____

7. keep _____ _____

_____

8. peep _____ _____

_____

9. team _____ _____

_____

10. seam _____ _____

_____

# Unit 9

1. like
2. fine
3. time
4. ice
5. ride
6. five
7. nice
8. hide
9. side
10. mile

These spelling words have the long *i* sound you hear in *ride*.

**A.** Write the spelling words that end with the letters **ide.**

1. _____  2. _____

3. _____

**B.** Write the words **five** and **fine.** There is one letter different in each word. Circle the letter that is different.

1. _____  2. _____

**C.** Write the spelling words that contain the letters **ice.**

1. _____  2. _____

**D.** Write the missing letters for these spelling words.

1. l ____ ____ ____  2. t ____ ____ ____

3. m ____ ____ ____

**E.** Write the spelling word that is a number word.

_____

**F.** Write the three letter spelling word.  _____

47

**A.** Write these spelling words in **a-b-c** order.

    like          ride          nice

    mile          side          time

1. _____   4. _____

2. _____   5. _____

3. _____   6. _____

**B.** Write the spelling word that goes with each meaning.

1. what a clock tells  _____

2. one more than four  _____

3. to put out of sight  _____

4. small and thin, very good  _____

5. frozen water  _____

Write the spelling word that belongs in each sentence.

1. The little boy was _____ years old.

2. Please put some _____ in my glass.

3. Jimmy is a very _____ person.

4. I _____ to eat cookies.

5. She walked one _____.

6. What _____ do you go to bed?

7. I like to sew with very _____ thread.

8. Would you like to _____ in my van?

9. The car had the numbers 777 on the _____.

10. Do you want to play _____ and seek?

Write the spelling words three times.

1. like _____  _____

   _____

2. fine _____  _____

   _____

3. time _____  _____

   _____

4. ice _____  _____

   _____

5. ride _____  _____

   _____

6. five _____  _____

   _____

7. nice _____  _____

_____

8. hide _____  _____

_____

9. side _____  _____

_____

10. mile _____  _____

_____

# Unit 10

1. toe
2. low
3. bow
4. hoe
5. sow
6. doe
7. rode
8. note
9. hole
10. joke

These words have the long *o* vowel sound you hear at the beginning of the word *oats*.

**A.** Write the spelling words that end with the letters **ow**.

1. _____   2. _____

3. _____

**B.** Write the spelling words that end with the letters **oe**.

1. _____   2. _____

3. _____

**C.** Write the spelling words that have the **o** + **consonant** + **e** spelling pattern.

1. _____   2. _____

3. _____   4. _____

**D.** Write the spelling words that begin with the letter **h**.

1. _____   2. _____

**E.** Write the spelling word that is a part of the body.

_____

**A.** Read the sentences. Write the spelling word that goes with each sentence.

1. This is a female deer. _____

2. This is the opposite of high. _____

3. This is attached to your foot. _____

4. This is something funny. _____

5. This is a short letter to someone. _____

6. This is a tool to use in a garden. _____

**B.** Write these words in **a-b-c** order.

    **sow**    **rode**    **bow**    **hole**    **hoe**

1. _____

2. _____

3. _____

4. _____

5. _____

Use spelling words to complete the sentences.

1. To plant a garden, first get a _____.

2. Dig a _____ and _____ the seed.

3. Push the dirt over the seed with your _____, then hope a _____ will not eat your plants.

4. If you see one, get a _____ and arrows.

5. Get down _____ so it will not see you.

6. Write a _____ telling it "This is not a _____, do not come back."

7. I saw some deer as we _____ up the road to the motel.

Write the spelling words three times.

1. toe  _____   _____

   _____

2. low  _____   _____

   _____

3. bow  _____   _____

   _____

4. hoe  _____   _____

   _____

5. sow  _____   _____

   _____

6. doe  _____   _____

   _____

7. rode _____ _____

_____

8. note _____ _____

_____

9. hole _____ _____

_____

10. joke _____ _____

_____

# Unit 11

1. know  2. mow

3. row  4. blow

5. snow  6. sold

7. gold  8. cold

9. told  10. old

These words have the long *o* sound. The long *o* sound can be spelled using the letter **o** when it is followed by the letters *ld*. The long **o** sound can also be spelled using the letters *ow*.

**A.** Write the spelling words that contain the letters **old**.

1. _____  2. _____

3. _____  4. _____

5. _____

**B.** Write the spelling words that end with the letters **ow**.

1. _____  2. _____

3. _____  4. _____

5. _____

**C.** Write the spelling word that belongs in each set.

1. tell and _____

2. sell and _____

**A.** Unscramble these spelling words.

1. dotl _____  2. sodl _____

3. ogld _____  4. nows _____

5. wolb _____  6. oldc _____

**B.** Write these words in **a-b-c** order.

    **mow**    **old**    **know**    **row**

1. _____  3. _____

2. _____  4. _____

**C.** Write the spelling word that sounds the same as **no**.

_____

**A.** Read the story. Write the spelling word that belongs in each sentence.

    You (1) _____ it is

(2) _____ weather when you see white

(3) _____ on the

ground. You would not want to (4) _____

the grass that day. You would not want to

(5) _____ a boat that day. The wind might

(6) _____ very hard and sound like an

(7) _____ man.

**B.** Write the word that goes with each meaning

    1. did tell _____

    2. did sell _____

    3. a yellow metal _____

Write the spelling words three times.

1. know _____ _____

   _____

2. mow _____ _____

   _____

3. row _____ _____

   _____

4. blow _____ _____

   _____

5. snow _____ _____

   _____

6. sold _____ _____

   _____

7. gold _____  _____

   _____

8. cold _____  _____

   _____

9. told _____  _____

   _____

10. old _____  _____

    _____

# Unit 12

# Time for Review tests

Ask your teacher for the tests.

# Unit 13

1. now
2. how
3. bow
4. cow
5. down
6. blew
7. few
8. grew
9. new
10. chew

Some of these words have the *ou* sound you hear in *out*. The sound is spelled by the letters *ow* as in *now*. Some of them have the *ü* sound of *u* as in the word *blue*. The sound is made by the letters *ew*.

**A.** Write the spelling words that end with **ow**.

1. _____  2. _____

3. _____  4. _____

**B.** Write the spelling words that end with **ew**.

1. _____  2. _____

3. _____  4. _____

5. _____

**C.** Look at the word pairs below. Some of the pairs have the same vowel sound. Write the pairs of spelling words that have the same vowel sound.

    how - cow         now - new

    bow - now         blew - few

1. _____  _____

2. _____  _____

3. _____  _____

**D.** Write the spelling word that is the opposite of **up**.

_____

**A.** Write the spelling word that goes with each meaning.

1. not old _____

2. at this time _____

3. to bend the head or body _____

4. what the wind did _____

5. what a tree did to be big _____

6. an animal that gives milk _____

**B.** Write the missing letters in these spelling words.

1. h _____ w

2. c _____ w

3. d _____ _____ n

4. gr _____ w

5. f _____ w

6. ch _____ w

Write the spelling word that belongs in each sentence.

1. Blowing bubbles is not a _____ game.

2. Many children like to _____ bubble gum.

3. Some have put a _____ pieces in their mouth at one time.

4. Do you know _____ to blow a big bubble?

5. One girl _____ a bubble that _____ bigger and bigger.

6. Some people move their mouth up and _____ so much while chewing, they look like a _____ chewing its cud.

7. If you win a bubble blowing contest, then you may _____ to your audience.

8. Does this story make you want some bubble gum _____?

68

Write the spelling words three times.

1. now _____ _____

_____

2. how _____ _____

_____

3. bow _____ _____

_____

4. cow _____ _____

_____

5. down _____ _____

_____

6. blew _____ _____

_____

7. few _____ _____

_____

8. grew _____  _____

   _____

9. new _____  _____

   _____

10. chew _____  _____

    _____

# Unit 14

1. day
2. way
3. say
4. may
5. pay
6. bake
7. lake
8. rake
9. wake
10. shake

    These words have the long *a* vowel sound you hear at the beginning of the word *ate*. In some words the long *a* sound is spelled with the letters *ay*. In others the long **a** sound is spelled by the *a* + **consonant** + *e* spelling pattern.

**A.** Write the spelling words that end with **ay**.

1. _____   2. _____

3. _____   4. _____

5. _____

**B.** Write the spelling words that rhyme with **bake**.

1. _____   2. _____

3. _____   4. _____

**C.** Vowels are left out of these words. Complete the words.

1. d _____ _____       2. b _____ k _____

3. w _____ _____       4. m _____ _____

5. r _____ k _____     6. sh _____ k _____

**A.** Write the spelling word that goes with each meaning.

1. to talk _____

2. big pond _____

3. the opposite of night _____

4. to cook in an oven _____

5. a tool used to gather leaves _____

**B.** Write these spelling words in **a-b-c** order.

**way    may    wake    shake    pay**

1. _____

2. _____

3. _____

4. _____

5. _____

Write the spelling word that belongs in each sentence.

1. The _____ was sunny.

2. It was a good day to _____ up early.

3. Let's go to the _____ and fish.

4. _____ we play in the water?

5. Please do not _____ no!

6. You can _____ a cake for us to take with us.

7. Which _____ should we go?

8. I hope we do not have to _____ to fish at the lake.

9. We will not need to gather leaves, so do not bring a _____ .

10. Do not _____ your line while you are waiting for a fish to bite the bait.

Write the spelling words three times.

1. day _____ _____

   _____

2. way _____ _____

   _____

3. say _____ _____

   _____

4. may _____ _____

   _____

5. pay _____ _____

   _____

6. bake _____ _____

   _____

7. lake _____ _____

   _____

8. rake _____  _____

   _____

9. wake _____  _____

   _____

10. shake _____

    _____

    _____

# Unit 15

1. sing
2. ring
3. king
4. wing
5. thing
6. fill
7. will
8. hill
9. bill
10. mill

Five of these spelling words rhyme with *swing*. They end with the letters *ing*. Five of them contain the word *ill*.

**A.** Write the spelling words that end with **ing**.

1. _____  2. _____

3. _____  4. _____

5. _____

**B.** Write the spelling words that end with **ill.**

1. _____  2. _____

3. _____  4. _____

5. _____

**C.** Write the spelling word that begins with the letter **s.**

_____

**D.** Write the spelling words that begin with the letter **w.**

1. _____  2. _____

**A.** Write these spelling words in **a-b-c** order.

    **will**          **ring**          **thing**          **mill**

1._____ 3. _____

2._____ 4. _____

**B.** Write the spelling word that goes with each meaning.

1. a bird's beak _____

2. a small mountain _____

3. a crowned ruler _____

4. to give a song _____

5. what a bird uses to fly _____

6. to put up to the top _____

Write the spelling word that belongs in each sentence.

1. A _____ has the shape of a circle.

2. Would you like to _____ a song?

3. _____ the cup to the top.

4. _____ you go to see the queen?

5. There was ice on the _____ of the plane.

6. We walked to the top of the _____.

7. Grain could be ground at the _____.

8. David became a _____ after he killed the giant.

9. Good _____s will happen if you love God.

10. The _____ of an eagle is bright yellow.

Write the spelling words three times.

1. sing _____  _____

   _____

2. ring _____  _____

   _____

3. king _____  _____

   _____

4. wing _____  _____

   _____

5. thing _____  _____

   _____

6. fill _____  _____

   _____

7. will _____  _____

   _____

8. hill _____  _____

_____

9. bill _____  _____

_____

10. mill _____  _____

_____

# Unit 16

1. bent
2. went
3. sent
4. tent
5. rent
6. hand
7. land
8. sand
9. and
10. stand

Five of these spelling words have the short *e* sound you hear in ***dent***. Five of these spelling words contain the word ***and***.

**A.** Write the spelling words that rhyme with **band.**

1. _____  2. _____

3. _____  4. _____

5. _____

**B.** Write the spelling words that end with **ent.**

1. _____  2. _____

3. _____  4. _____

5. _____

**C.** Add **s** to these spelling words to form plurals.

1. tent _____

2. land _____

**D.** Write the spelling words that begin with the letter **s.**

1. _____  2. _____

3. _____

**A.** Write these spelling words in **a-b-c** order.

went    sent    and    tent    bent

1. _____    4. _____

2. _____    5. _____

3. _____

**B.** Write the spelling words that have these two meanings.

1. to give to; a part of the body  _____

2. to touch shore; dirt  _____

**C.** One word in each set is not spelled correctly. Write the word correctly.

1. sent, reant, bent  _____

2. sande, hand, and  _____

3. rent, land, stande  _____

**A.** Write the spelling word that fits each clue.

1. a part of the body _____

2. something found at the beach _____

3. a place to sleep outside the home _____

4. dented _____

**B.** Write the spelling word that belongs in each sentence.

5. James _____ Kevin went to fix the car.

6. Please _____ by me.

7. The house was for _____.

8. The plane did not _____ safely.

9. I _____ to the store before school.

10. He _____ a letter to me.

Write the spelling words three times.

1. bent _____ _____

   _____

2. went _____ _____

   _____

3. sent _____ _____

   _____

4. tent _____ _____

   _____

5. rent _____ _____

   _____

6. hand _____ _____

   _____

7. land _____ _____

   _____

8. sand _____  _____

   _____

9. and _____  _____

   _____

10. stand _____

    _____

    _____

# Unit 17

1. call
2. ball
3. tall
4. fall
5. all
6. well
7. bell
8. fell
9. sell
10. yell

Five of these spelling words contain the word *all*. Five of these spelling words contain the short *e* sound you hear in *tell*.

**A.** Write the spelling words that contain the word **all** in them.

1. _____  2. _____

3. _____  4. _____

5. _____

**B.** Write the spelling words that end with the letters **ell**.

1. _____  2. _____

3. _____  4. _____

5. _____

**C.** Write the word that names each picture.

1. _____

2. _____

**D.** Circle the word that does not belong in each set.

1. ball     dog     cat     2. well     sick     ill

Write the spelling word that goes with each meaning.

1. a deep hole that holds water _____

2. to give for money _____

3. something that rings _____

4. not short _____

5. to scream loudly _____

6. a round toy _____

7. every bit of something _____

8. to have fallen _____

9. to slip and come down _____

10. something you can do on a phone _____

Write the spelling word that belongs in each sentence.

1. The baby liked to bounce the _____.

2. Jesus loves _____ the people of the world.

3. It was time for the _____ to ring.

4. Lie down if you do not feel _____.

5. _____ your teacher if you can not be at school.

6. The baby goat was not _____.

7. We would like to _____ the house to someone.

8. The woman was not hurt badly when she _____.

9. It is not nice to _____ at people.

10. Leaves turn colors in the _____ season.

Write the spelling words three times.

1. call _____ _____

   _____

2. ball _____ _____

   _____

3. tall _____ _____

   _____

4. fall _____ _____

   _____

5. all _____ _____

   _____

6. well _____ _____

   _____

7. bell _____ _____

   _____

8. fell _____ _____

   _____

9. sell _____ _____

   _____

10. yell _____ _____

    _____

# Unit 18

# Time for Review tests

Ask your teacher for the tests.

# Unit 19

1. sled
2. slip
3. slide
4. sleep
5. slow
6. plate
7. place
8. plan
9. plane
10. plus

A consonant cluster is a set of letters whose sounds are blended so closely together that they almost make one sound. The *sl* in *sleep* and the *pl* in *plane* are consonant clusters.

**A.** Write the spelling words that begin with the consonant cluster **sl.**

1. _____  2. _____

3. _____  4. _____

5. _____

**B.** Write the spelling words that begin with the consonant cluster **pl.**

1. _____  2. _____

3. _____  4. _____

5. _____

**C.** Write the missing consonant cluster to complete each word.

1. _____ _____ eep     2. _____ _____ ace

3. _____ _____ ow      4. _____ _____ us

**A.** One word is not spelled correctly in each set.
   Write the word correctly.

1. place     sleap     slip  _____

2. slede     slide     plan  _____

3. slipe     place     slide _____

**B.** Write the spelling word that goes with each meaning.

1. a thing to ride in for flying _____

2. a thing to put food on _____

3. a thing to use in snow _____

4. the sign used when adding numbers_____

5. an idea of how to do something _____

6. not fast _____

7. to put something in its spot _____

8. to move smoothly over a surface _____

Write a spelling word to complete each sentence.

1. Two _____ two equals four.

2. The boy went down the _____.

3. Please put my _____ in the sink.

4. It is easy to _____ down on ice.

5. _____ your fork on the table.

6. A _____ can slide fast on snow.

7. Sometimes it is hard to go to _____ when you are excited.

8. A _____ flies over our house.

9. Please _____ down; do not drive so fast.

10. What do you _____ to do after school?

Write the spelling words three times.

1. sled  _____  _____

   _____

2. slip  _____  _____

   _____

3. slide  _____  _____

   _____

4. sleep  _____  _____

   _____

5. slow  _____  _____

   _____

6. plate  _____

   _____

   _____

7. place _____

_____

_____

8. plan _____  _____

_____

9. plane _____

_____

_____

10. plus _____  _____

_____

# Unit 20

1. bring	2. brown

3. brave	4. broke

5. brick	6. truck

7. try	8. tree

9. trip	10. true

    A consonant cluster is a set of letters whose sounds are blended so closely together that they almost make one sound. The **br** in **bring** and the **tr** in **tree** are consonant clusters.

**A.** Write the spelling words that begin with the consonant cluster **tr.**

1. _____  2. _____

3. _____  4. _____

5. _____

**B.** Write the spelling words that begin with the consonant cluster **br.**

1. _____  2. _____

3. _____  4. _____

5. _____

**C.** Add the ending to these words. Write the new words.

1. brave + ly _____

2. try + ing _____

**D.** Add **s** to each word to make it mean more than one.

1. trip _____

2. brick _____

**A.** One word in each set is not spelled correctly. Find the misspelled word and write it correctly.

1. broun    brave    truck _____

2. true     brok     brave _____

3. tree     bring    trie _____

4. truk     trip     brick _____

5. brown    bringe   broke _____

**B.** Write the spelling word that goes with each meaning.

1. a tall plant _____

2. having courage _____

3. not false _____

4. a journey _____

5. something used to make houses _____

Read the story. Write the spelling word that belongs in each sentence.

If you are (1) _____ enough, you can (2) _____ to climb a (3) _____.

Do not take a red (4) _____ with you.

You can not drive a (5) _____ on this

(6) _____ up the tree. You can

(7) _____ a lunch in a

(8) _____ bag.

**B.** Use the code to find each spelling word.

$b = 1$     $e = 2$     $k = 3$     $o = 4$

$r = 5$     $t = 6$     $u = 7$

1. $1 + 5 + 4 + 3 + 2$   _____

2. $6 + 5 + 7 + 2$   _____

Write the spelling words three times.

1. bring _____ _____

   _____

2. brown _____ _____

   _____

3. brave _____ _____

   _____

4. broke _____ _____

   _____

5. brick _____ _____

   _____

6. truck _____ _____

   _____

7. try _____ _____

   _____

8. tree _____ _____

_____

9. trip _____ _____

_____

10. true _____ _____

_____

# Unit 21

1. green    2. grin

3. grass    4. grow

5. gray     6. free

7. frog     8. from

9. front    10. friend

These words begin with the consonant clusters *gr* and *fr*.

**A.** Write the spelling words that begin with the consonant cluster **fr.**

1. _____  2. _____

3. _____  4. _____

5. _____

**B.** Write the spelling words that begin with the consonant cluster **gr.**

1. _____  2. _____

3. _____  4. _____

5. _____

**C.** Write the spelling words that contain double letters.

1. _____  2. _____

3. _____

**D.** Write the spelling words that name a color.

1. _____  2. _____

**A.** Write these spelling words in **a-b-c** order.

| gray | frog | green | front | grass |
|---|---|---|---|---|
| friend | grin | free | grow | from |

1._____ 6. _____

2._____ 7. _____

3._____ 8. _____

4._____ 9. _____

5._____ 10._____

**B.** Write the spelling word that goes with each meaning.

1. the color of grass _____

2. a green animal that hops _____

3. the opposite of back _____

4. a little smile _____

Write spelling words to complete the story.

Once upon a time in the little town of Fairdale there lived a little (1) _____. It was sitting on the sidewalk in the (2) _____ of the Kays's house. Mr. Kays thought it was cute and wanted to take a picture of it. It sat perfectly still like it was his (3) _____. It could have hopped into the green (4) _____, but it did not seem to want to get away (5) _____ him. It was as if it had a (6) _____ on its face while getting its picture taken. It surely didn't think Mr. Kays was a frog because its skin was (7) _____, and his hair was (8) _____. After the picture was taken, it was (9) _____ to hop away and eat bugs, so it could (10) _____ bigger.

Write the spelling words three times.

1. green _____ _____

   _____

2. grin _____ _____

   _____

3. grass _____ _____

   _____

4. grow _____ _____

   _____

5. gray _____ _____

   _____

6. free _____ _____

   _____

7. frog _____  _____

   _____

8. from _____  _____

   _____

9. front _____

   _____

   _____

10. friend _____

    _____

    _____

# Unit 22

1. ship
2. shoe
3. sheep
4. shell
5. show
6. shop
7. shine
8. shape
9. shore
10. shade

The letters **sh** make the sound you hear at the beginning of *she*. The *sh* is called a **consonant digraph**. All of these spelling words begin with the *sh* consonant digraph.

**A.** Write the spelling words that have five letters in them.

1. _____  2. _____

3. _____  4. _____

5. _____  6. _____

**B.** Write the spelling word that rhymes with **hop.**

_____

**C.** Write the spelling word that rhymes with **bow.**

_____

**D.** Write the spelling word that names each picture.

1. _____

2. _____

3. _____

**A.** Write the spelling word that goes with each meaning.

1. a foot covering _____

2. an animal whose fur is wool _____

3. another word for beach _____

4. to let someone see something _____

5. a small store _____

6. a covering to stay out of the sun _____

**B.** Unscramble these words.

1. psahe _____

2. nihse _____

3. lehsl _____

**C.** Write the spelling word that has these two meanings.

1. a large boat; 2. to send a package _____

Write the spelling word that belongs in each sentence.

1. The sun will _____ today.

2. The large _____ was named Titanic.

3. A rectangle is a _____.

4. We walked along the _____.

5. The _____ was too small for my foot.

6. Please _____ me how to play the game.

7. A big tree will give a lot of _____.

8. A baby _____ is called a lamb.

9. You can find a _____ on the beach.

10. You may buy a tire for your bike at the bike _____.

Write the spelling words three times.

1. ship _____ _____

   _____

2. shoe _____ _____

   _____

3. sheep _____ _____

   _____

4. shell _____ _____

   _____

5. show _____ _____

   _____

6. shop _____ _____

   _____

7. shine  _____

_____

_____

8. shape  _____

_____

_____

9. shore  _____

_____

_____

10. shade _____

_____

_____

# Unit 23

1. think
2. tenth
3. thing
4. theft
5. math
6. thud
7. with
8. Seth
9. thorn
10. bath

The words in this unit contain the consonant digraph *th*. The ***th*** sounds like the beginning of the word *the*.

**A.** Write the spelling words that begin with the consonant digraph **th**.

1. _____  2. _____

3. _____  4. _____

5. _____

**B.** Write the spelling words that end with the consonant digraph **th**.

1. _____  2. _____

3. _____  4. _____

5. _____

**C.** Write the spelling words that rhyme with **path**.

1. _____  2. _____

**D.** Write the spelling word that starts with a capital letter.

_____

**A.** Entry words in a dictionary are listed in **a-b-c** order. Look at each pair of words. Write the spelling word that would come between these words in a dictionary.

1. **bad** _____ **bed**

2. **this** _____ **those**

3. **wind** _____ **wobble**

4. **tent** _____ **term**

**B.** Write the word that goes with each meaning.

1. to use your mind _____

2. stealing _____

3. a boy's name _____

4. having to do with numbers _____

5. a dull sound _____

6. an object _____

**A.** Use spelling words to complete the sentences.

1. _____ can be easy if you use your brain and _____.

2. I did not want to get stuck with a _____ for the _____ time.

3. If you stink, take a _____.

4. _____ was the boy that was singing.

5. I heard a _____ when the tree fell.

**B.** Use the code to write spelling words.

e = 1    f = 2    g = 3    h = 4

i = 5    n = 6    t = 7    w = 8

1. 7 + 4 + 5 + 6 + 3 = _____

2. 8 + 5 + 7 + 4 = _____

3. 7 + 4 + 1 + 2 + 7 = _____

Write the spelling words three times.

1. think  _____  _____

   _____

2. tenth  _____  _____

   _____

3. thing  _____  _____

   _____

4. theft  _____  _____

   _____

5. math  _____  _____

   _____

6. thud  _____  _____

   _____

7. with _____  _____

_____

8. Seth _____  _____

_____

9. thorn_____

_____

_____

10. bath _____

_____

_____

# Unit 24

# Time for Review tests

Ask your teacher for the tests.

# Unit 25

1. doing
2. going
3. wanting
4. growing
5. washing
6. blowing
7. falling
8. looking
9. wishing
10. walking

You can make new words by adding *ing* to words you already know. All of these words have the *ing* ending.

**A.** Add **ing** to these base words to make spelling words.

1. go  2. look  3. wash  4. want  5. do

6. wish  7. fall  8. blow  9. walk  10. grow

1. _____  2. _____

3. _____  4. _____

5. _____  6. _____

7. _____  8. _____

9. _____  10. _____

**B.** Write the spelling words that have double letters.

1. _____  2. _____

**C.** Write the spelling words that have the long **o** sound spelled **ow**.

1. _____  2. _____

**A.** Write these spelling words in **a-b-c** order.

| wanting | blowing | doing | going |
|---------|---------|-------|-------|
| falling | walking | growing | wishing |

1._____  5._____

2._____  6._____

3._____  7._____

4._____  8._____


**B.** Write the spelling word that goes with each meaning.

1. cleaning          _____

2. seeing            _____

3. getting bigger _____

4. slipping          _____

Write the spelling word that belongs in each sentence.

1. The wind was _____ very hard.

2. We were _____ home.

3. We were _____ at the trees.

4. Trees began _____.

5. We were not _____ the power to go out.

6. We were not _____ for a blackout.

7. It was not safe to be _____ in the woods.

8. It was not a good time to be _____ your car.

9. The wind was _____ a good job of blowing things around.

10. It was not a time to be thinking of _____ vegetables.

Write the spelling words two or three times each.

1. doing _____ _____

2. going _____ _____

3. wanting_____

_____

_____

4. growing _____

_____

5. washing _____

_____

_____

6. blowing _____

_____

_____

7. falling _____

_____

_____

8. looking _____

_____

_____

9. wishing_____

_____

_____

10. walking _____

_____

_____

# Unit 26

1. boys
2. girls
3. cats
4. birds
5. pets
6. trees
7. books
8. dogs
9. ants
10. bugs

A word that names a person, place, or thing is called a **noun**. You can make some nouns mean more than one by adding an **s** to the end of the word.

**A.** Write these nouns to make them mean more than one.

1. bird  2. boy  3. book  4. ant  5. tree

1. _____  2. _____

3. _____  4. _____

5. _____

**B.** Write the spelling words that name animals.

1. _____  2. _____

3. _____  4. _____

5. _____  6. _____

**C.** Write the spelling words that relate to people.

1. _____  2. _____

**D.** Write the spelling words that have double vowels.

1. _____  2. _____

**E.** Write the spelling words that contain **ir**.

1. _____  2. _____

**A.** Write the spelling word that goes with each clue.

1. more than one pet _____

2. more than one girl _____

3. more than one book _____

4. more than one tree _____

**B.** Write these words in **a-b-c** order.

| boys | cats | birds | books |
| dogs | ants | bugs  |       |

1. _____   5. _____

2. _____   6. _____

3. _____   7. _____

4. _____

Write the spelling word or words that belong in each sentence.

1. The _____ and _____ made bird feeders.

2. Some _____ were flying north.

3. The woman had many _____ meowing.

4. He did not climb all the _____.

5. Many _____ were in the library.

6. _____ are bugs that like to eat sweet things.

7. I do not like _____ in my kitchen.

8. There were several _____ barking.

9. Some people like to have many kinds of _____.

Write the spelling words three times.

1. boys _____  _____

   _____

2. girls _____  _____

   _____

3. cats _____  _____

   _____

4. birds _____  _____

   _____

5. pets _____  _____

   _____

6. trees _____  _____

   _____

7. books _____  _____

   _____

8. dogs _____  _____

_____

9. ants _____  _____

_____

10. bugs _____  _____

_____

# Unit 27

1. looks
2. rides
3. plays
4. sleeps
5. makes
6. jumps
7. sees
8. rakes
9. walks
10. runs

Words such as **run**, **walk**, and **skip** show action. An action word is called a **verb**. These spelling words are verbs. An *s* has been added to form a new word.

**A.** Add **s** to each verb. Write the new word.

   1. see          2. make          3. ride

   4. play         5. rake          6. jump

1. _____    2. _____

3. _____    4. _____

5. _____    6. _____

**B.** Write the spelling words that have double vowels.

1. _____    2. _____

3. _____

**C.** Write the spelling word that rhymes with **talks.**

_____

**D.** Write the spelling word that rhymes with **buns.**

_____

**A.** Write the spelling word that goes with each meaning.

1. hops up and down _____

2. looks _____

3. rests at night _____

4. gathers leaves _____

**B.** Write these spelling words in **a-b-c** order.

| **makes** | **walks** | **plays** |
|---|---|---|
| **looks** | **rides** | **runs** |

1. _____  4. _____

2. _____  5. _____

3. _____  6. _____

Write the spelling word that belongs in each sentence.

1. He _____ in the soft bed.

2. She _____ in the van.

3. Victoria _____ home made cookies.

4. Debbie _____ on the treadmill.

5. Beverly _____ the leaves with a rake.

6. Lynn _____ the pretty flowers.

7. Clarence _____ at the babies.

8. David _____ on the trampoline.

9. Jimmy _____ with the bat and ball.

10. He _____ to first base.

Write the spelling words three times.

1. looks _____ _____

   _____

2. rides _____ _____

   _____

3. plays _____ _____

   _____

4. sleeps _____ _____

   _____

5. makes _____ _____

   _____

6. jumps _____ _____

   _____

7. sees _____ _____

_____

8. rakes _____

_____

_____

9. walks _____

_____

_____

10. runs _____ _____

_____

# Unit 28

1. looked
2. wished
3. helped
4. played
5. snowed
6. jumped
7. called
8. showed
9. walked
10. brushed

**Verbs** are action words. Often you can add *ed* to verbs when you want to say that something has already happened.

**A.** Add **ed** to these base words to make them show something has already happened.

    1. snow      2. play      3. jump

    4. walk      5. help      6. wish

1. _____    2. _____

3. _____    4. _____

5. _____    6. _____

**B.** Write the spelling words that have double letters.

1. _____    2. _____

**C.** Write the spelling words that have the **sh** consonant digraph.

1. _____    2. _____

3. _____

**A.** Write the spelling word that goes with each meaning.

1. saw _____

2. took part in a game _____

3. pointed out something _____

4. hoped _____

**B.** Write these spelling words in **a-b-c** order.

    jumped        helped        snowed

    walked        brushed       called

1. _____

2. _____

3. _____

4. _____

5. _____

6. _____

Write the spelling word that belongs in each sentence.

1. It had _____ several inches.

2. He stood and _____ at the snow.

3. We _____ to the grocery.

4. The children _____ in the snow.

5. Someone _____ us how to make a snow angel.

6. The dog _____ in the snow.

7. She _____ snow off her coat.

8. Lynn _____ her mother on the phone.

9. We _____ for warm weather.

10. James _____ her shovel snow.

Write the spelling words two or three times each.

1. looked _____  _____

2. wished _____  _____

3. helped _____

_____

4. played _____

_____

5. snowed _____

_____

_____

6. jumped _____

_____

_____

7. called _____

_____

_____

8. showed _____

_____

_____

9. walked _____

_____

_____

10. brushed _____

_____

_____

# Unit 29

1. I'm
2. I'll
3. can't
4. let's
5. that's
6. we're
7. he's
8. she's
9. it's
10. don't

These spelling words are called contractions. **Contractions** are two words put together, but part of one word is left out. *I'm* is a contraction. It is made from the words *I* and *am*. The *a* in *am* is not used. This mark (') is called an **apostrophe**. An apostrophe is used in the place of the missing letter or letters.

**A.** Write the contraction that is made of each pair of words.

1. I am _____

2. let us _____

3. he is _____

4. can not _____

5. I will _____

6. we are _____

**B.** Write the contractions in which **'s** stands for the word **is**.

1. _____  2. _____

3. _____  4. _____

**C.** Vowels are missing in these contractions. Fill in the missing vowels.

1. d _____ n't    2. _____ t's    3. sh _____ 's

**D.** Write the contractions in which the word **not** was shortened.

1. _____  2. _____

**E.** Write the contractions in which a capital **I** was used.

1. _____  2. _____

One word in each set is not spelled correctly. Write the word correctly.

1. I'm     thit's     can't _____

2. A'll     he's     we're _____

3. we're     ha's     don't _____

4. I'll     she's     I'n _____

5. lat's     we're     that's _____

6. cen't     it's     don't _____

7. let's     I'll     shi's _____

8. I'm     we'ra     can't _____

9. dan't     he's     I'll _____

10. let's     we're     at's _____

Read the story.  Write the spelling word that belongs in each sentence.  The first letter is given.

(1) L_____ take a trip to the zoo.  You

(2) c_____ force an elephant to eat ice cream.

We (3)(d)_____ want to get into the lion's cage.

(4) I_____ just too dangerous.  (5) I_____

planning on having a good time watching the monkeys.

(6) T_____ a fun thing to do.  Mable wanted to

go.  If she gets to go, (7) s_____ going to have a

good time.  If James gets to go, (8) h_____ going

to have a good time too.  (9) W_____ looking

forward to having a good time.  (10) I_____ be

the driver.

154

Write the spelling words three times.

1. I'm  _____  _____

   _____

2. I'll  _____  _____

   _____

3. can't  _____  _____

   _____

4. let's  _____  _____

   _____

5. that's  _____  _____

   _____

6. we're  _____  _____

   _____

7. he's _____ _____

_____

8. she's _____

_____

_____

9. it's _____ _____

_____

10. don't _____

_____

_____

# Unit 30

# Time for Review tests

Ask your teacher for the tests.

# Unit 31

1. food
2. boot
3. soon
4. zoo
5. room
6. do
7. cool
8. pool
9. noon
10. school

These spelling words have the same vowel sound you hear in *too* and *moon*. This sound is often spelled *oo* as in *soon*. Sometimes it is spelled with one *o* as in the word *to*.

**A.** Write the spelling words that end with the **oo** sound.

1. _____  2. _____

**B.** Write the spelling words that end with the letter **l**.

1. _____  2. _____

3. _____

**C.** Write the spelling words that end with the letter **n**.

1. _____  2. _____

**D.** Vowels are missing in these spelling words. Write them correctly.

1. f ____ ____ d    2. b ____ ____ t    3. r ____ ____ m

**A.** Write the spelling word that goes with each meaning.

1. something you wear on your foot _____

2. a place to see animals _____

3. before long _____

4. a place to swim _____

5. a place to learn _____

6. the middle of the day _____

7. a little cold _____

**B.** Write these spelling words in **a-b-c** order.

    food        room        do        school

1. _____

2. _____

3. _____

4. _____

Write the spelling word that belongs in each sentence. You will need to add *s* to one word.

1. Children go to _____ to learn.

2. We can go on a field trip to the _____.

3. We can watch polar bears swim in a _____.

4. We should not feed the animals any _____.

5. It is fun to watch penguins in their _____.

6. The weather should be _____ in October.

7. We will not have to wear our _____.

8. The children _____ like to go on field trips.

9. We should go _____.

10. Will we be back by _____?

Write the spelling words three times.

1. food _____ _____

_____

2. boot _____ _____

_____

3. soon _____ _____

_____

4. zoo _____ _____

_____

5. room _____ _____

_____

6. do _____ _____

_____

7. cool _____  _____

   _____

8. pool _____  _____

   _____

9. noon _____  _____

   _____

10. school _____

    _____

    _____

# Unit 32

1. car
2. far
3. dark
4. arm
5. star
6. for
7. or
8. corn
9. torn
10. horn

The letters *ar* spell the **r-controlled** vowel sound you hear in *car*. The letters *or* spell the **r-controlled** vowel sound you hear in *fork*.

**A.** Write the spelling words that have the *or* vowel sound.

1. _____  2. _____

3. _____  4. _____

5. _____

**B.** Write the spelling words that have the *ar* vowel sound.

1. _____  2. _____

3. _____  4. _____

5. _____

**C.** Write the spelling word that names something you can drive.

_____

**D.** Write the spelling word that names something you can eat.

_____

**E.** Write the spelling word that names a part of the body.

_____

**A.** Write the spelling word that means the opposite of each of these words.

1. near _____   2. light _____

**B.** Write the words that sound the same as these words.

1. oar _____

2. four _____

**C.** Write the spelling word that goes with each meaning.

1. ripped _____

2. something you can eat _____

3. a part of the body _____

4. something you can drive _____

5. something that shines at night _____

6. a trumpet _____

Write the spelling word that belongs in each sentence.

1. At night the sky is _____.

2. The zoo is not very _____ away.

3. I love to eat _____ on the cob.

4. Do you like milk _____ juice?

5. The _____ on the car works now.

6. The woman changed into another dress because her other one was _____.

7. I ironed the shirt _____ him.

8. James's _____ was bruised.

9. The North _____ is bright.

10. Kevin drove a blue _____.

Write the spelling words three times.

1. car  _____  _____

   _____

2. far  _____  _____

   _____

3. dark  _____  _____

   _____

4. arm  _____  _____

   _____

5. star  _____  _____

   _____

6. for  _____  _____

   _____

7. or _____ _____

_____

8. corn _____ _____

_____

9. torn _____ _____

_____

10. horn _____ _____

_____

# Unit 33

1. wish  2. fish

3. wash  4. brush

5. dash  6. with

7. path  8. teeth

9. both  10. tooth

These spelling words end with the consonant digraphs *sh* or *th*.

**A.** Write the spelling words that end with **sh.**

1. _____  2. _____

3. _____  4. _____

5. _____

**B.** Write the spelling words that end with **th.**

1. _____  2. _____

3. _____  4. _____

5. _____

**C.** Write the spelling words that have five letters.

1. _____  2. _____

3. _____

**D.** Write the spelling word that names each picture.

_____  _____

**A.** Entry words in a dictionary are listed in **a-b-c** order. Look at each pair of words. Write the spelling word that would come between these words in a dictionary.

1. **fast** _____ **foot**

2. **them** _____ **two**

3. **bath** _____ **bread**

4. **damp** _____ **desk**

5. **witch** _____ **wood**

**B.** Write the word that goes with each meaning.

1. to want something _____

2. a small trail to walk on _____

3. to clean something _____

4. more than one tooth _____

5. something used to clean teeth _____

Use spelling words to finish the list of things you could do on a camping trip.

1. Catch a _____.

2. Walk along a _____.

3. _____ dishes in a stream.

4. Wear shoes on _____ feet.

5. Brush _____ with spring water.

6. Swim _____ a friend.

7. _____ my hair.

8. _____ down a path to the lake.

9. Don't break a _____ in my mouth.

10. _____ I could stay longer.

Write the spelling words three times.

1. wish _____ _____

   _____

2. fish _____ _____

   _____

3. wash _____ _____

   _____

4. brush _____ _____

   _____

5. dash _____ _____

   _____

6. with _____ _____

   _____

7. path _____  _____

_____

8. teeth _____  _____

_____

9. both _____  _____

_____

10. tooth _____

_____

_____

# Unit 34

1. to
2. too
3. two
4. be
5. bee
6. their
7. there
8. they're
9. see
10. sea

Two words that sound the same but are not spelled alike are called **homophones**. *To,* *too,* and *two* are homophones. They sound alike but are not spelled alike and do not mean the same thing.

Write the spelling word that does not belong in each group.

1. their, be, they're _____

2. bee, two, to _____

3. their, two, there _____

4. they're, there, see _____

5. their, they're, too _____

6. to, see, sea _____

7. be, they're, bee _____

8. to, their, two _____

9. see, there, sea _____

10. to, see, sea _____

Write the spelling word that goes with each meaning.

1. contraction for they are _____

2. also _____

3. belonging to them _____

4. to exist _____

5. in that place _____

6. to look _____

7. a number _____

8. large body of water _____

9. as far as _____

10. an insect _____

Circle the correct homophone that belongs in each sentence.

1. Did you ever watch a (be, bee) at work?

2. It gets nectar from flowers and takes it back (to, two, too) the hive.

3. (Their, There, They're) are many bees in a hive.

4. Bees make wax from a place in (their, there, they're) bodies.

5. (Their, There, They're) not found much near the (see, sea).

6. The bees feed and care for the queen (to, two, too).

7. There can only (be, bee) one queen in each hive, not (to, two, too).

8. Would you like to (see, sea) the queen bee?

Write the spelling words three times.

1. to  _____  _____

   _____

2. too  _____  _____

   _____

3. two  _____  _____

   _____

4. be  _____  _____

   _____

5. bee  _____  _____

   _____

6. their  _____  _____

   _____

7. there _____

_____

_____

8. they're _____

_____

_____

9. see _____  _____

_____

10. sea _____  _____

_____

# Unit 35

1. birthday
2. cowboy
3. outside
4. herself
5. himself
6. myself
7. airplane
8. sunset
9. bedroom
10. mailbox

A **compound word** is a word made of two words. *Sunset* is a compound word. It is made from the words *sun* and *set*.

Write the compound word that is made from each pair of words.

1. birth + day _____

2. air + plane _____

3. sun + set _____

4. out + side _____

5. cow + boy _____

6. bed + room _____

7. mail + box _____

8. her + self _____

9. my + self _____

10. him + self _____

**A.** Write the spelling word that goes with each meaning.

1. something to ride in that flies _____

2. a man who rides in a rodeo _____

3. when the sun goes down _____

4. the day a person is born

   _____

5. a room for sleeping _____

6. the opposite of inside _____

7. a box in which to receive mail

   _____

**B.** Write these spelling words in **a-b-c** order.

    herself        myself        himself

1. _____

2. _____

3. _____

Match the words in Row 1 and Row 2 to make compound words.

| Row 1 | Row 2 | |
|---|---|---|
| 1. birth | plane | _____ |
| 2. sun | side | _____ |
| 3. her | boy | _____ |
| 4. cow | self | _____ |
| 5. mail | set | _____ |
| 6. out | self | _____ |
| 7. air | day | _____ |
| 8. my | room | _____ |
| 9. bed | self | _____ |
| 10. him | box | _____ |

Write the spelling words two times.

1. birthday _____

   _____

2. cowboy _____

   _____

3. outside _____

   _____

4. herself _____

   _____

5. himself _____

   _____

6. myself _____

   _____

7. airplane _____

   _____

8. sunset _____

   _____

9. bedroom_____

   _____

10. mailbox_____

    _____

# Unit 36

# Time for Review tests

Ask your teacher for the tests.

# Alphabet Chart

| | | | |
|---|---|---|---|
| A a | B b | C c | D d |
| E e | F f | G g | H h |
| I i | J j | K k | L l |
| M m | N n | O o | P p |
| Q q | R r | S s | T t |
| U u | V v | W w | X x |
| Y y | Z z | | |

# Spelling Glossary Pronunciations

ă cat map

ā age, race

ä father, calm

ã care, air

ĕ red, bed

ē eat, he

ė mother, heard

ĭ is, it

ī ice, ride

ŏ hot, cot

ō over, go

ô ball, caught

ô order, pour

oi oil, boy

ou house, out

öö brook, look

ŭ up, cup

ū use, few

ü rule, move

ə represents

a in about

e in taken

i in pencil

o in lemon

u in circus

## A a

**airplane** (ãr ' plān) a machine that flies and is driven by a motor.
We saw the airplane fly overhead.

**all** (ôl) the whole thing
She ate all the cookie.

**and** (ănd) added to, also
I like apples and carrots.

**arm** (ärm) the part of the body between the shoulder and the hand.
My arm had a bruise on it.

**ate** (āt) did eat
I ate the pudding.

## B b

**bake** (bāk) to cook in an oven
She likes to bake a cake.

**ball** (bôl) a round toy
Ben likes to play with a ball.

**bath** (băth) a washing of the body
Take a bath to get your body clean.

**beam** (bēm) a ray of light
The sun sends beams of light.

**bed** (bĕd) a thing to sleep on
I slept in the bed.

**bedroom** (bĕd – rüm) a room in which to sleep.

**be** (bē) to exist; to live

**bee** (bē) an insect that makes honey and wax
You can get honey from a bee hive.

**bell** (bĕl) a metal cup that makes a musical sound

**bent** (bĕnt) curved
He bent the wire over.

**big** (bĭg) large
An eagle is a big bird.

**bill** (bĭl) the mouth of a bird
A bird eats with its bill.

**bird** (bėrd) an animal with wings and feathers. pl *birds*
A swallow is a small bird.

**birthday** (bėrth – dā) the day on which a person was born.

**bled** (blĕd) did bleed
His cut finger bled a lot.

**blew** (blü) did blow
The wind blew my hair.

**blimp** (blĭmp) an airship
There was a big blimp floating across the sky.

**blot** (blŏt) a spot or stain
There was a blot on the fabric.

**blow** (blō) send forth a current of air
**blowing**
The wind can blow the leaves.

**book** (böök) many printed pages put together to be read. pl. *books*
I read the book of John Bunyan.

**boot** (büt) a covering for the foot.
Jimmy put his foot in the boot.

**boss** (bŏs) one who is in control of others
The teacher is the boss of the class.

**both** (bōth) the two together
I wore both shoes.

**bow** (bō) a weapon for shooting arrows
You can shoot a deer with a bow and arrow.
**bow** (bou) to bend the body in a greeting or reverence

**box** (bŏks) a wood, paper, or metal container to put things in

# boy

**boy** (boi) male child from birth to eighteen years old. *pl. boys*

**brag** (brăg) to speak too highly of one's self
The girl liked to brag about what she had done.

**brave** (brāv) without fear, having courage.
It is not easy to be brave if you meet a bear in the woods.

**brick** (brĭk) a block of clay baked by fire.
The house had red bricks on it.

**brim** (brĭm) the topmost edge of a cup
Fill the cup almost to the brim.

**bring** (brĭng) to take something to a place
What did you bring to our house today?

**broke** (brōk) did break
I broke a glass bowl.

**brown** (broun) a dark color like that of coffee.
The dog was chocolate brown.

**brush** (brŭsh) a thing used to fix hair
**brushed**
Brush your hair every morning.

**buck** (bŭk) a male deer
I think someone killed a buck.

## C c

**call** (kôl) speak loudly, cry or shout
**called**
Listen closely for the teacher to call your name.

**came** (kām) did come
James came home from work.

**can't** (kănt) a contraction for can not.

**car** (kär) a vehicle that moves on four wheels.
I drove the car home.

**cat** (kăt) a small furry pet that catches mice *pl. cats*

# crush

**chew** (chü) to crush or grind with the teeth.
Please chew your food with your mouth closed.

**chin** (chĭn) the part of the face below the mouth
Men should shave their chin.

**chop** (chŏp) to cut into small pieces
You can chop onion for your burger.

**clap** (klăp) to strike the hands together

**clot** (klŏt) a thick mass of blood
Your blood should clot quickly.

**club** (klŭb) a heavy stick
The club could hurt someone.

**cold** (kōld) not hot, less warm
Winters are cold in Alaska.

**cool** (kül) somewhat cold; more cold than hot.
It was a cool morning.

**corn** (kôrn) a yellow grain that grows on large ears.
We had corn for supper yesterday.

**cost** (kŏst) the amount of money
How much did the dress cost?

**cow** (kou) a dairy animal that furnishes milk.

**cowboy** (kou′ boi) a man who looks after cattle on a ranch.
There is not much need of cowboys since people put up fences.

**crest** (krĕst) the top of a hill

**crop** (krŏp) food that is grown
I hope we have a large crop of cucumbers.

**crush** (krŭsh) to press or squeeze hard enough to break

## D d

**dark**(därk) having no light
It was dark outside at midnight.

**dash**(dăsh) splash or throw
Just put a dash of salt on the beans.

**day**(dā) the time between sunrise and sunset.
It is light outside during the day.

**disk** (dĭsk) something round and flat that can be used to store information

**do**(dü) to work until the job is finished
**doing**
I try do the job well.

**doe** (dō) a female deer

**dog**(dôg) *pl. dogs* a four-legged pet used to guard the house.
The dog barks loudly.

**don't**(dōnt) a contraction for do not.
I don't want to meet a lion in the forest.

**down**(doun) in a lower place.
I went down to Tennessee.

**drag** (drăg) to move along slowly
Please drag the chair to the other side.

**dust** (dŭst) small pieces of dirt
Please wipe the dust from the bookcase.

**dwell** (dwĕl) to stay for a while in one place
We can dwell in this state for a long time.

## F f

**fall**(fôl) to drop from a higher place
**falling**

**far**(fär) a long way
Texas is far away from Kentucky.

**fast** (făst) speedy
We were moving at a fast pace.

**feed** (fēd) give food to
Did he feed the cattle?

**fell**(fĕl) past tense of fall.
I almost fell down on the porch.

**few** (fyoō) a small number of
We had a few cups left.

**fill**(fĭl) to put in until there is no more room.
Fill the glass to the top.

**fine**(fīn) 1)small and thin. 2)very good
She did a fine job on the cake.

**fish**(fĭsh) an animal that lives in water
Frankie had fish in an aquarium.

**fit**(fĭt) make right or proper
She fixed the dress to fit her.

**five**(fīv) one more than four
The baby was five months old.

**flag** (flăg) a rectangular piece of cloth that is used to represent a nation
Our flag has red and white stripes.

**flat** (flăt) having a smooth, level surface
The top of the printer was flat.

**fled** (flĕd) did flee
She fled after the dog bit the boy.

**floss**(flŏs) a string used to clean between the teeth
Make sure you use floss to keep from having cavities.

**food**(füd) anything that people eat.
Vegetables are good food to eat.

**for**(fôr) in consideration of
I got ice cream for him.

**free**(frē) 1) loose, not fastened, 2) costing nothing.
We got the pudding free if we bought three others.

# friend

**friend**(frĭnd) a person who knows and likes another person.

**frog**(frŏg) a small green jumping animal with webbed feet.
The frog was sitting on the sidewalk.

**from**(frŏm) out of
We went away from Indiana.

**front**(frŭnt) the first part
Have you read the front of the book?

**fuss**(fŭs) to complain about something
Sometimes I fuss about James's driving.

## G g

**game**(gām) a way of playing
We played the Candy Land game.

**gate**(gāt) an opening in a fence
The gate was left open.

**gave**(gāv) past tense of give
I gave the boy some candy.

**girl**(gėrl) a female child *pl. girls*

**go**(gō) to move along; **going**
We were going on vacation.

**gold**(gōld) a heavy, bright yellow precious metal
The street in Heaven is gold.

**grass**(grăs) the green blades that cover lawns
James mowed the grass.

**gray**(grā) a color obtained when mixing black and white
He wore gray pants.

**green**(grēn) the color of many growing plants and grass
She wore a green blouse.

**grew**(grü) past tense of grow
He grew three inches.

**grin**(grĭn) a broad smile
Please grin when getting your picture taken.

# hush

**grow**(grō) to become bigger; **growing**
Aaron should grow more.

## H h

**hand**(hănd) the end part of the arm which holds objects

**help**(hĕlp) to aid someone; **helped**
Will you help me with washing dishes?

**herself**(hėr sĕlf´) used to make a statement stronger for a female.
Missie herself was upset about the teacher's attitude.

**he's**(hēz) contraction for he is
He's such an active child.

**hide**(hīd) put out of sight.
It is fun to play hide-and-seek.

**hill** ((hĭl) a raised part of the earth

**himself**((hĭm sĕlf´) used to make a statement stronger for a male.
He himself was tired of sitting in the waiting room.

**hoe** (hō) a tool with a long handle and a small blade across the end used for cutting weeds

**hole**(hōl) open place
Do not fall in the hole.

**home**(hōm) the place where a person lives
My home is in Fairdale.

**hope**(hōp) a desire for something
I hope Clarence will get home early.

**horn**(hôrn) 1)a hard growth on the head of some cattle 2) a musical instrument
The boy played the horn beautifully.

**how**(hou) in what way
How do you bake a cake?

**hush** (hŭsh) to be quiet
You can hush your mouth.

## I i

**ice**(īs) frozen water
Ice cubes will make a drink cold.

**I'll**(īl) contraction for I will
I'll read some more later.

**I'm**(īm) contraction for I am
I'm planning to go to see Monica.

**it's**( ĭts) contraction for it is
It's a nice day.

## J j

**joke**(jōk) something said to make someone laugh
Lee likes to tell jokes to make us laugh.

**jump**(jŭmp) to spring up from something
**jumps**; **jumped**
The boys like to jump on the trampoline.

## K k

**keep**(kēp) to have for a long time
I will keep the old book for a while.

**king**(kĭng) a man who rules a country
King David was liked by his people.

**know**(nō) to be able to tell apart from others
I did not know who Betty was.

## L l

**lake**(lāk) a body of water surrounded by land
We went fishing at Tom Wallace Lake.

**land**(lănd) 1)the solid part of the earth's surface 2) to touch shore
We own the land on which our house is built.

**left** (lĕft) the opposite of right
Some people write with their left hand.

**less**(lĕs) fewer
I weigh less than Richard.

**let's**(lĕts) contraction for let us
Let's get something to eat.

**like**(līk) much the same as
Byron looks like Kevin.

**limp** (lĭmp) to walk with difficulty
I walked with a limp when my knee was hurting.

**look**(löök) to see
**looked, looking, looks**
I would like to look at the speaker.

**lost** (lŏst) not found
The key was lost.

**low** (lō) not high

## M m

**made**(mād) past tense of make
I made some cookies.

**mailbox**(māl ' bŏks) a box from which mail is collected
I have already gotten the mail from the mailbox today.

**mash** (măsh) to crush
We can mash potatoes after they are boiled.

**make**(māk) bring into being
**makes**
I would like to make a hat for Abigail.

**match** (măch) a piece of wood with a composition that catches fire easily
James used a match to start a fire.

**math** (măth) the study of numbers

**may**(mā) an asking word used for asking permission to do something
May I get an apple?

**me**(mē) a pronoun referring to one's self.

# mess

**mess** (mĕs) a jumble
Do not leave a mess in your room.

**mile** (mīl) a unit of measure, a long way

**mill** (mĭl) the building containing a machine for grinding wheat
Please go to the mill to get some wheat flour.

**mow** (mō) to cut down grass
I like to mow grass with a riding lawn mower.

**must** (mŭst) a necessity
We must eat and sleep.

**myself** (mī sĕlf ′) a word used to make a statement stronger about one's self
I myself want to lose weight.

## N n

**name** (nām) a word or words by which a person or thing is called
What is your name?

**need** (nēd) to be in want
I need a drink.

**new** (nü) never used
I would like some new black shoes.

**nice** (nīs) something that is pleasing
I have a nice blue dress that fits me well.

**noon** (nün) 12 o'clock in the day
I ate my sandwich before noon.

**nose** (nōz) the part of the face used for smelling
I can smell food with my nose.

**note** (nōt) a short letter

**now** (nou) at this time
I need to stop now to fix supper.

## O o

**old** (ōld) not young
Mae was more than one hundred years old.

**or** (ôr) Or suggests a choice
I would like a pizza or a taco.

**outside** (out ′ sīd) the side that is out
The man left the package outside.

## P p

**path** (păth) a way made for people or animals to walk upon
God made a dry path through the Red Sea.

**pay** (pā) to give money for things or work
I wanted to get my pay for the two days I worked.

**peep** (pēp) the cry of a young chick

**place** (plās) a portion of space

**plan** (plăn) a thing that is detailed telling what to do

**plane** (plān) a vehicle for traveling in air

**plate** (plāt) a flat dish

**play** (plā) something done to amuse oneself **plays; played**
I like to play kickball with Jimmy and David.

**plug** (plŭg) an electrical device with prongs
Please do not let the plug fall into water.

**plus** (plŭs) a sign used for adding

**pool** (pül) a small body of water in which to play
The boys like to get into the pool.

**press** (prĕs) to push against
I press down on the keyboard keys.

## R r

**rake** (rāk) *pl. rakes* a long handle tool having teeth at the other end.

**read** (rēd) get the meaning of
You can read a book.

**rent**(rĕnt) a regular payment for the use of property

**ride**(rīd) to sit in or on something while it is moving  **rides**
I plan to ride in the van to town.

**ring**(rĭng) a circle or band that goes around something
Put a ring around the correct answer.

**rode**(rōd) did ride
I rode in the red car to church.

**room**(rüm) a part of a house
The toys are in the front room.

**row**(rō) 1)a line of people or things; 2)to use oars to move a boat
Quickly row the boat to the shore.

**run**(rŭn) to move the legs quickly  **runs**

**rust** (rŭst) a reddish-brown coating on steel that has been exposed to air and moisture
The truck had much rust on it.

## S s

**safe**(sāf) free from danger
Please keep the baby safe for me.

**sand**(sănd) tiny grains of worn-down rock.
There was much sand along the shore.

**say**(sā) speak
Will Kevin say the names of the presidents?

**school**(skül) a place for teaching and learning
I hope you like to go to school.

**sea**(sē) a large body of salt water smaller than the ocean
I have never seen the Mediterranean Sea.

**seam**(sēm) the line formed by sewing two pieces of cloth together
I sewed a seam in my skirt.

**see** (sē) to look at
I can see the moon sometimes at night.

**seed**(sēd) a thing from which a plant grows
James planted cucumber seeds in his garden.

**sell**(sĕl) to exchange for money

**sent**(sĕnt) did send
The shipment was sent the next day.

**Seth**( sĕth) a boy's name
One of Adam's sons was named Seth.

**shade**(shād) partly dark; not in sunshine
There was shade under the tree.

**shake**(shāk) to move quickly backwards and forwards

**shape**(shāp) form; figure
A cube is in the shape of a square.

**shed** (shĕd) a small building for storage

**sheep**(shēp) an animal raised for wool and mutton
David took care of his father's sheep.

**shell**(shĕl) the hard outside covering of an animal
We walked along the shore and picked up shells.

**she's** (shēs) contraction for she is

**shine**(shīn) to send out light.
Let the light shine on your book so you can see well enough to read.

**ship**(shĭp) a large boat
The ship sank to the bottom.

**shoe**(shü) an outer covering for the foot

**shop**(shŏp) a place where things are sold
She was in her craft shop.

# shore

**shore**(shôr) land at the edge of a sea
We walked along the shore and picked up shells.

**show**(shō) let be seen
**showed**

**side**(sīd) a border of an object
The title was on the side of the book.

**sing**(sĭng) to make music with the voice
I love to sing and play the piano.

**skim** (skĭm) 1)to read quickly over something; 2) low-fat milk
You can skim over the page instead of reading all of it.
I like to drink skim milk.

**slap** (slăp) a hit with the palm of the hand
Do not slap me in the face.

**sled** (slĕd) a thing to carry people or things over snow or ice

**sleep**(slēp) to rest body and mind
**sleeps**
I like to sleep in the recliner.

**slip** (slĭp) to unintentionally slide for a short distance

**slow** (slō) not fast

**snow**(snō) soft white frozen moisture that falls from the sky
**snowed**
We did not have much snow last winter.

**so**(sō) in that way
Please use the microphone so you can be heard.

**sold**(sōld) past tense of sell
We sold the piano.

**soon**(sün) in a short time
He should call soon.

**sow** (sō) to put seed in the ground
What kind of seed did he sow?

# their

**spot**(spŏt) a small part that is different
There were colored spots on her jumper.

**stand**(stănd) to be upright on one's feet
Please stand until you are ask to be seated.

**star**(stär) a heavenly body appearing as a bright point in the sky at night time
Can you see the North Star?

**step** (stĕp) a single movement of the foot in walking

**sunset**( sŭn' sĕt) the going down of the sun.

**swim** (swĭm) to glide along in water
Brian could swim well.

## T t

**take**(tāk) to lay hold of
Please take your keyboard with you.

**tall**(tôl) higher than the average
Vickie is not very tall.

**team**(tēm) number of people working together

**teeth**(tēth) more than one tooth
Brush your teeth every day.

**tenth** (tĕnth) next one after the ninth

**tent**(tĕnt) a moving shelter made of cloth
The people of Israel lived in tents.

**thank**(thăngk) a way that someone shows they are pleased or grateful
You should always say, "Thank you," when someone does a favor for you.

**that**(thăt) a word used to point out something

**that's** (thăts) contraction for that is

**theft** (thĕft) stealing

**their**(thãr) belonging to them
That white truck is their truck.

# them

**them**(thĕm) the persons or objects spoken of

**then**(thĕn) at that time
Will you go with us then?

**there**(thãr) in that place
Set the book there.

**these**(thēz) used to point out more than one person, thing, or idea
Put these papers in the binder.

**they**(thā) people, things, or ideas spoken about
Do you know how they play the piano?

**they're**(thãr) contraction for they are
They're going to be in the room.

**thick**(thĭk) not thin, much space from one side to the other
The big book was thick.

**thin**(thĭn) not thick, not much space from one side to the other
The paper was thin.

**thing**(thĭng) any object
A pen is a thing.

**think**(thĭnk) to use the brain

**this**(thĭs) a word used to point out one thing or person
This light is bright.

**thorn** (thorn) a sharp pointed woody point sticking out from a stem

**those**(thōz) a word used to point out more than one person or thing
Those boxes all look alike.

**thud** (thŭd) a dull sound

**time**(tīm) all the days there have ever been or will ever be
What time were you born?

**to**(tü) in the direction of
Go to the door.

**toe** (tō) one of the end parts of the foot

# weed

**told**(tōld) past tense of tell
I told him he could go.

**too**(tü) also
I told Donna she could go too.

**tooth**(tüth) a hard bonelike part in the mouth used for biting or chewing
I chipped my tooth.

**torn**(tôrn) past tense of tear
The dress was torn.

**tree**(trē) *pl. trees* the largest kind of plants with a woody trunk

**trip** (trĭp) a journey from one's home for fun

**truck** (trŭk) a large motor vehicle for carrying things

**true** (trü) not false, not a lie

**try** (trī) to make an effort to do something

**two**(tü) one more than one
I have two white shoes.

## W w

**wake**(wāk) to stop sleeping
I usually wake up early.

**walk**(wôk) to go on both feet
**walked, walking, walks**
I like to walk for exercise.

**want**(wônt) to wish for
**wanting**
I want to eat some cookies.

**wash**(wôsh) to clean with water
**washing**
James can wash the dishes.

**way**(wā) a manner or style
Which way do you comb your hair?

**weed**(wēd) a troublesome plant
James pulled weeds from his garden.

**week**

**week**( wēk) seven days Sunday – Saturday
We stayed in Indiana for almost one week.

**well**(wĕl) (1) a hole bored in the ground from where one can get water (2) not sick

**wind** (wĭnd) air in motion

**wing**(wĭng) the part of a bird used for flying

**wish**(wĭsh) to desire to have **wished wishing**
I wish I could win a lot of money.

**zoo**

**went**(wĕnt)) did go
We went to church yesterday evening.

**we're** (wē ėr) contraction for we are

**will**(wĭl) am going to
I will get the clothes.
**with**(wĭth) a word that shows two or more things are together

## Y y

**yell**(yĕl) to cry out with a loud voice

## Z z

**zoo**(zü) a place where wild animals are kept and shown for many people to view
We went to the zoo on Kevin's birthday.

# Unit 6 Test
## Part 1

Circle the correct spelling of the word that belongs in the blank.

1. How _____ can you run?

    A. fasst	B. fast	C. fest

2. Do not _____ anyone.

    A. slap	B. slapp	C. slep

3. Hold your paper _____.

    A. flate	B. flat	C. flatt

4. Our _____ is red, white, and blue.

    A. flagg	B. flage	C. flag

5. We should not _____ on ourselves.

    A. bragg	B. brage	C. brag

6. Do not _____ on a snake.

    A. step	B. stepp	C. stap

7. Do you know how to _____?

    A. swime	B. swim	C. swimm

8. I hope we have a big _____ of tomatoes.

    A. croop	B. cropp	C. crop

9. We _____ get some sleep.

    A. must	B. musst	C. muust

10. Byron said to turn _____.

    A. lefft          B. lef          C. left

11. I like to drink _____ milk.

    A. skiim          B. skim          C. skimm

12. Use _____ to help clean your teeth.

    A. floss          B. flos          C. floos

# Unit 6 Test
## Part 2

Circle the correct spelling of the word that belongs in the blank.

1. Please _____ your hair.

    A. bruch	B. brash	C. brush

2. _____ your pencil onto your paper.

    A. Press	B. Prass	C. Pres

3. A strong _____ can blow a tree down.

    A. winde	B. wend	C. wind

4. Was there a _____ on the shirt?

    A. blott	B. blot	C. blote

5. The truck has _____ on it.

    A. russt	B. rust	C. rast

6. The mower was in the blue _____.

    A. shed	B. shad	C. shedd

7. You can listen to music on a compact _____.

    A. disc	B. dissk	C. disk

8. Did the clothes _____ much?

    A. coost	B. cost	C. cosst

9. Fill the cup to the _____.

    A. brim	B. brimm	C. brin

10. Do not touch the _____ if your hands are wet.

    A. plog                   B. plug                 C. plugg

11. The spilled milk was a _____.

    A. mess                B. mes                C. mese

12. There was a _____ of paint on the shirt.

    A. spoot                B. spott              C. spot

# Unit 6 Test
## Part 3

Circle the correct spelling of the word that belongs in the blank.

1. Adam was made from the _____ of the earth.

    A. dust                B. dustt               C. dusst

2. If you can not lift the box, _____ it.

    A. dragg               B. drag                C. drage

3. I weigh _____ than she does.

    A. lees                B. less                C. lese

4. Men should shave their _____.

    A. chin                B. chinn               C. chine

5. Someone _____ the key.

    A. loust               B. losst               C. lost

6. James made his own _____.

    A. clubb               B. cluub               C. club

7. Do we have a _____ to start a fire?

    A. mach                B. match               C. mattch

8. I saw the _____ in the sky.

    A. blimp               B. blemp               C. blimmp

9. Do you have your own _____?

    A. shup                B. shopp               C. shop

10. You can _____ grapes to make grape juice.

    A. cruss                     B. crush                  C. cush

11. I _____ down the driveway after the dog bit the boy.

    A. flad                      B. fled                    C. fledd

12. There was a _____ stream of water.

    A. thinn                    B. thinne                C. thin

13. Was the _____ at work today?

    A. boss                     B. boos                  C. bos

14. A male deer is called a _____.

    A. buc                       B. buk                    C. buck

Unit 6 Test
Part 4

Circle the correct spelling of the word that belongs in the blank.

1. _____ your hands when you sing.

   A. Clapp            B. Clap            C. Cllap

2. His arm _____ onto his sleeve.

   A. bled            B. blede            C. bledd

3. We should want to _____ in the house of the Lord.

   A. dweel            B. dwel            C. dwell

4. Matt is our _____.

   A. frend            B. frind            C. friend

5. She can learn to _____ potatoes.

   A. mach            B. mash            C. massh

6. I hope her blood was able to _____.

   A. clot            B. cloot            C. clott

7. _____ your mouth to stay out of trouble.

   A. Huch            B. Hush            C. Hushe

8. Did you know _____ woman?

   A. thaat            B. thatt            C. that

9. Did you walk to the _____ of the hill?

   A. crest            B. crist            C. krest

10. Was the dog walking with a _____?

    A. limp                       B. lemp                   C. limmp

11. _____ some nuts and put them in a cake.

    A. Chup                   B. Shop                 C. Chop

12. The baby began to _____.

    A. fus                         B. fuss                     C. fess

# Unit 12 Test
## Part 1

Circle the correct spelling of the word that belongs in the blank.

1. Can you write your last _____?

    A. neam            B. name            C. nam

2. I _____ supper.

    A. ate             B. aet             C. atae

3. Hide-and-seek is a fun _____.

    A. gamm            B. game            C. geam

4. Would you _____ me to the zoo?

    A. tack            B. taek            C. take

5. Riding on a four-wheeler might not be _____.

    A. safe            B. saffe           C. saef

6. We _____ cookies at school.

    A. maed            B. maid            C. made

7. We can _____ some again.

    A. mack            B. make            C. maek

8. We _____ to live right if we want to go to Heaven.

    A. nead            B. nede            C. need

9. James _____ me the key.

    A. gaev            B. gave            C. gavve

10. I want to _____ it.

    A. keep          B. keap          C. kepe

11. He _____ here after he left his job.

    A. kame         B. came         C. camm

12. A mustard _____ is very little.

    A. sede          B. sead          C. seed

Unit 12 Test
Part 2

Circle the correct spelling of the word that belongs in the blank.

1. I would _____ to ride my bike.

    A. like            B. licke           C. liek

2. I am not _____ years old.

    A. fife            B. five            C. fiev

3. It was a _____ day to go riding.

    A. nise            B. nies            C. nice

4. I should walk a _____ every day.

    A. mill            B. miel            C. mile

5. It is not _____ cold outside.

    A. ice             B. ise             C. isce

6. What _____ is it?

    A. tiem            B. time            C. tim

7. It was a _____ time to go riding.

    A. fine            B. fin             C. fien

8. Who would like to _____ a horse?

    A. feed            B. fead            C. fede

9. The story was no _____.

    A. jock            B. joke            C. jocke

10. Is that a _____ or a flower?

    A. weed                  B. wead                C. wede

11. My _____ was hurting.

    A. sied                  B. sid                  C. side

12. I did not run and _____.

    A. hidde               B. hide                C. hid

# Unit 12 Test
## Part 3

Circle the correct spelling of the word that belongs in the blank.

1. There is _____ weather in winter.

    A. cold          B. kold          C. colde

2. You will not need to _____ grass during the winter.

    A. mowe          B. moew          C. mow

3. There might be _____ on the ground.

    A. snoe          B. snow          C. snoa

4. Sometimes there will be a cool wind that will _____.

    A. blowe         B. blow          C. bloae

5. You would not want to _____ a boat on a lake in the winter.

    A. row           B. rowe          C. roaw

6. The children _____ to school in the van.

    A. rodde         B. roed          C. rode

7. The teacher _____ the children about Heaven.

    A. tode          B. toad          C. told

8. The street is pure _____.

    A. goad          B. gold          C. golde

9. We all should _____ about Heaven.

    A. now           B. knoe          C. know

10. No one will grow _____ in Heaven.

    A. old                        B. olde                   C. ode

11. Nothing will be _____ in Heaven.

    A. sold                    B. solde                C. soad

12. You will not have to write a _____ to your teacher in Heaven.

    A. noat                 B. note                 C. nolte

# Unit 12 Test
## Part 4

Circle the letter of the correct spelling for the word that belongs in the blank.

1. Please close the _____ .

    A. gate          B. gat          C. gaet

2. I got up and began to _____ my bike again.

    A. ried          B. ride         C. ridde

3. A _____ of light from the sun is bright.

    A. beme          B. beem         C. beam

4. There will be no _____ in your shoes there.

    A. hoal          B. hoel         C. hole

5. My _____ was bruised.

    A. toa           B. toe          C. tooe

6. He wants to _____ seed in the ground.

    A. sow           B. soe          C. soa

7. Have you heard a baby chick _____?

    A. pepe          B. peap         C. peep

8. Lie _____ on the floor.

    A. low           B. loa          C. loo

9. She ripped the _____ in her dress.

    A. seme          B. seam         C. saem

10. He tied the belts into a _____.

    A. bou          B. bow          C. boe

11. Was the deer a _____ or a buck?

    A. doe          B. dow          C. doa

12. Richard was a player on the _____.

    A. teem          B. teme          C. team

13. He used a _____ to cut the weeds.

    A. ho          B. hoa          C. hoe

14. Would you like to _____ a book to me?

    A. read          B. reid          C. rede

Unit 18 Test
Part 1

Circle the correct spelling of the word that belongs in the blank.

1. A baby _____ is a calf.

   A. cow          B. cowe          C. cou

2. Jimmy got a _____ toy helicopter.

   A. neue         B. newe          C. new

3. We should not _____ to other gods.

   A. bou          B. bow           C. bowe

4. The flowers _____ up quickly.

   A. grue         B. greu          C. grew

5. January 1 is the first _____ of the year.

   A. dae          B. day           C. daay

6. We went _____ to Donna's house.

   A. down         B. doun          C. done

7. We should _____ our food well.

   A. choo         B. chew          C. chewe

8. We should never _____ bad words.

   A. saey         B. saiy          C. say

217

9. We have a _____ pieces of candy.

   A. few          B. foo          C. feu

10. God's _____ is always best.

    A. way         B. waey         C. waye

11. _____ old are you?

    A. Howe        B. Houe         C. How

12. The wind _____ hard against the van.

    A. blew        B. bloo         C. blwe

13. _____ I eat lunch?

    A. Mae         B. May          C. Maye

14. _____ I can quit.

    A. Nou         B. Now          C. Nowe

Unit 18 Test
Part 2

Circle the correct spelling of the word that belongs in the blank.

1. Do not _____ the cup to the top.

   A. feil            B. file            C. fill

2. We should always _____ our bills.

   A. pay            B. paye            C. paey

3. _____ the milk bottle so the chocolate will mix with the milk.

   A. Shaek            B. Shake            C. Shack

4. Benjamin tries to _____ "Jesus Loves Me."

   A. seng            B. sinj            C. sing

5. We can _____ leaves in the fall.

   A. rack            B. raek            C. rake

6. Some birds will act like they have a hurt _____.

   A. wing            B. winng            C. weng

7. It is fun to _____ cookies.

   A. back            B. bake            C. backe

8. Let the phone _____ two times.

   A. ringg            B. ring            C. reng

219

9. Would you like to go to the _____ to catch some fish?

    A. lake                B. lack               C. lakee

10. It is a very good _____ to learn to read.

    A. theng            B. thingg           C. thing

11. Please do not _____ the baby.

    A. wack            B. wake            C. waek

12. We use the _____ James Version Bible.

    A. King              B. Keing           C. Kingg

Unit 18 Test
Part 3

Circle the correct spelling of the word that belongs in the blank.

1. Putting up the _____ was a hard job.

    A. tint	B. tent	C. tennt

2. The boys liked to play in the _____.

    A. sannd	B. send	C. sand

3. _____ you go to church with me?

    A. Wil	B. Will	C. Wiel

4. One giant had six fingers on each _____.

    A. hand	B. hannd	C. hend

5. It looked like the pipes were _____.

    A. bent	B. bennt	C. bint

6. The hospital _____ might be high.

    A. beil	B. bil	C. bill

7. Mara _____ home early.

    A. wint	B. went	C. wennt

8. We wanted to buy some _____.

    A. lend	B. lande	C. land

9. I do not like to drive up that _____.

    A. hill          B. heal          C. hile

10. Kayla was glad to _____ the house.

    A. rint          B. rent          C. rente

11. Have you ever been to a flour _____?

    A. mill          B. mile          C. mil

12. Patti _____ Kevin out of the room.

    A. sint          B. sennt          C. sent

# Unit 18
## Part 4

Circle the correct spelling of the word that belongs in the blank.

1. Ring the _____ for service.

    A. bale             B. bel              C. bell

2. _____ still while you are getting your picture taken.

    A. Stand            B. Stannd           C. Stend

3. Do not _____ in the classroom.

    A. yeel             B. yell             C. yill

4. Be careful not to _____ down.

    A. faal             B. fall             C. faul

5. You may _____ your mother on the phone.

    A. cal              B. caul             C. call

6. I hope Earl is feeling _____ soon.

    A. well             B. will             C. wele

7. David did not drink _____ of his milk.

    A. aul              B. awl              C. all

8. Tyrel _____ and hurt his head.

    A. fel              B. fell             C. feel

9. Many babies like to play with a _____.

    A. ball                B. balle            C. boll

10. Isaiah _____ Noah were singing loudly.

    A. an                B. and             C. annd

11. We wanted to _____ the piano.

    A. sele             B. sel              C. sell

12. How _____ are you?

    A. tall               B. toll             C. taul

# Unit 24 Test
## Part 1

Circle the correct spelling of the word that belongs in the blank.

1. Two _____ two equals four.

    A. pluse            B. pluus            C. plus

2. You should stay away from roads when riding on a _____.

    A. sled             B. slead            C. slede

3. Have you ever been on a UPS _____?

    A. plaen            B. plane            C. plaan

4. I am _____ when getting on my bike.

    A. slou             B. slow             C. slowe

5. It is easy to _____ and fall when walking on ice.

    A. slipe            B. slep             C. slip

6. What was the name of the _____?

    A. plase            B. plaes            C. place

7. Most small children enjoy going down a _____.

    A. slide            B. slid             C. slied

8. What is your _____ for today?

    A. plann            B. plan             C. plen

9. I would like to _____ some more.

    A. sleep             B. slepe             C. sleap

10. I like to use the blue _____.

    A. plaet             B. plate             C. plat

11. Please _____ me some ice water.

    A. breng            B. brang            C. bring

12. A _____ bear would not make a good pet.

    A. brown           B. broun           C. brouwn

# Unit 24 Test
## Part 2

Circle the correct spelling of the word that belongs in the blank.

1. Always tell _____ stories.

    A. treu             B. true             C. truw

2. I rode in the back of James's _____.

    A. truck            B. truk             C. truke

3. The church had red _____ on it.

    A. briek            B. breck            C. brick

4. Please _____ to do your best.

    A. try              B. trie             C. trei

5. The sky is not _____.

    A. grean            B. green            C. grene

6. What color is _____?

    A. grase            B. graas            C. grass

7. To be a hero, you must be _____.

    A. brav             B. brave            C. braeve

8. Would you like to climb a _____?

    A. trea             B. tree             C. treae

9. Who _____ the lid to the candle holder?

    A. broke                  B. broak                C. brock

10. I did not want to go on the _____.

    A. tripe                  B. trep                 C. trip

11. Can you make the baby _____?

    A. grin                   B. gren                 C. grine

12. Babies _____ a lot during their first two years of life.

    A. groe                  B. grou                 C. grow

# Unit 24 Test
## Part 3

Circle the correct spelling of the word that belongs in the blank.

1. Mix the colors black and white to make _____.

    A. gray	B. grey	C. graye

2. The _____ sat on the sidewalk.

    A. froge	B. froog	C. frog

3. The puppies were _____.

    A. frea	B. free	C. frey

4. It is too far for you to walk home _____ school.

    A. from	B. frome	C. frum

5. Did you see my _____, Teresa?

    A. freind	B. friend	C. frend

6. Go to the _____ door of the house.

    A. frunt	B. front	C. font

7. The large _____ hit an iceberg.

    A. ship	B. shep	C. shipe

8. David took care of his father's _____.

    A. shepe	B. sheap	C. sheep

9. A small store is called a _____.

    A. shop          B. shoop          C. shope

10. Please do not walk with your _____ lace untied.

    A. shue          B. shoo          C. shoe

11. A circle is a round _____.

    A. shap          B. shaap          C. shape

12. You can look for a _____ in the sand.

    A. shele          B. shell          C. sheel

13. Open the curtains and let the sun _____ in the room.

    A. shine          B. shing          C. shien

14. _____ the puppy to the little girl.

    A. Showe          B. Show          C. Shoa

# Unit 24 Test
## Part 4

Circle the correct spelling of the word that belongs in the blank.

1. The tree fell with a _____.

   A. thud           B. thuud          C. thad

2. Janie and I ran along the _____ together.

   A. shore          B. shure          C. shoer

3. Do you _____ we can take a nap?

   A. thingk         B. think          C. thik

4. _____ and Summer were the singers.

   A. Sethe          B. Sech           C. Seth

5. Will you go _____ me to the store?

   A. with           B. witth          C. withe

6. Her birthday was the _____ of May.

   A. tinth          B. teth           C. tenth

7. After playing in dirt, Ben needed a _____.

   A. bathe          B. bath           C. baath

8. Name one _____ you want for your birthday.

   A. thang          B. theng          C. thing

9. We could sit under the _____ of that big tree.

   A. shade            B. shede            C. shaid

10. The man had committed a _____.

   A. theft             B. thefft           C. thevt

11. I had tried to teach _____ to Don.

   A. mathe           B. maeth           C. math

12. I was stuck by a _____.

   A. thorne          B. thorn           C. thurn

# Unit 30 Test
## Part 1

Circle the correct spelling of the word that belongs in the blank.

1. The wind was _____ the van.

    A. blowing         B. blouing         C. bloweng

2. I had been _____ to get exercise.

    A. wallking         B. waulkeng         C. walking

3. Andrew was _____ he would win some money.

    A. weshing         B. wiching         C. wishing

4. Donna has three _____.

    A. boyes         B. boys         C. boyse

5. Beverly _____ leaves in her yard.

    A. raiks         B. rakes         C. raeks

6. I _____ on the internet for David's picture.

    A. looked         B. lookt         C. louked

7. _____ a pretty day.

    A. Its'         B. It's         C. Ite's

8. How many _____ are in your yard?

    A. trees         B. treas         C. tress

9. She _____ well in the recliner.

    A. slleeps          B. sleaps          C. sleeps

10. Mother _____ me on the phone.

    A. cauled          B. called          C. calld

11. _____ go into the water if you see a whale.

    A. Doon't          B. Don't          C. Dont'

12. There are many _____ in the library.

    A. bukks          B. buks          C. books

13. A kangaroo _____ high.

    A. jumps          B. jamps          C. jumpps

14. The car was stuck because it has _____ so much.

    A. snooed          B. snowd          C. snowed

Unit 30 Test
Part 2

Circle the correct spelling of the word that belongs in the blank.

1. We were _____ the red car.

    A. woshing      B. washing      C. washeng

2. _____ you ride a bike?

    A. Can't      B. Cann't      C. Cant'

3. Patti has three _____.

    A. doggs      B. doges      C. dogs

4. Ben _____ in the car seat.

    A. rids      B. rides      C. riddes

5. We _____ kickball with the boys.

    A. plaid      B. playd      C. played

6. _____ planning to be a teacher.

    A. I'm      B. Iam'      C. I'me

7. Matt was _____ his homework.

    A. doeng      B. doing      C. duing

8. Mike has two _____.

    A. cates      B. cattes      C. cats

9. Byron _____ into his room.

    A. runs          B. runns          C. runes

10. Vickie _____ Matt with his homework.

    A. helpped          B. helped          C. hellped

11. _____ a silver car.

    A. That's          B. Thet's          C. Thatt's

12. I was _____ a cookie.

    A. wonting          B. wantong          C. wanting

# Unit 30 Test
## Part 3

Circle the correct spelling of the word that belongs in the blank.

1. James _____ good French fries.

    A. maeks          B. mackes          C. makes

2. We were _____ to church.

    A. going          B. goeng           C. goeing

3. I do not like _____ in my kitchen.

    A. antes          B. ants            C. annts

4. Sarah _____ her hair.

    A. brushd         B. brushed         C. brusht

5. _____ not been sleeping much.

    A. He's           B. Hes'            C. Hie's

6. Snow was _____ in the yard.

    A. fauling        B. fawling         C. falling

7. I do not want any _____ .

    A. pets           B. petts           C. petes

8. She _____ on the treadmill.

    A. wallks         B. walks           C. waulks

9. _____ go get some lunch.

    A. Lett's          B. Lets'          C. Let's

10. Vickie _____ they could go on vacation.

    A. wishd          B. wished          C. weshed

11. _____ not going to have school on Saturday.

    A. We're          B. Wee're          C. We' er

12. The boys _____ on the trampoline.

    A. jumpped          B. jumped          C. jumppd

Unit 30 Test
Part 4

Circle the correct spelling of the word that belongs in the blank.

1. Weeds were _____ in our garden.

    A. groweing        B. groweng        C. growing

2. There were many _____ at camp.

    A. girls        B. grils        C. girles

3. Sue _____ the piano well.

    A. playes        B. plays        C. plase

4. Abigail _____ at the toys.

    A. luks        B. lookes        C. looks

5. _____ a sweet little baby.

    A. Shee's        B. She's        C. Shes'

6. Jimmy _____ me his bike.

    A. showed        B. shooed        C. showd

7. Some _____ were eating bread in our yard.

    A. berds        B. burds        C. birds

8. I _____ to the corner.

    A. wallked        B. walked        C. walkeed

9. _____ sing a song.

    A. I'ill        B. Ill'        C. I'll

10. She _____ better with glasses.

    A. seas        B. sees        C. seez

11. I do not like _____ in my house.

    A. bugs        B. buggs        C. bugz

12. Monica was _____ at the toys.

    A. looking        B. louking        C. lookeng

# Unit 36
## Part 1

Circle the correct spelling of the word that belongs in the blank.

1. What kind of _____ do you like best?

    A. foud　　　　　　B. food　　　　　　C. fude

2. I like _____ on the cob.

    A. corn　　　　　　B. curn　　　　　　C. corrn

3. The grandmother had false _____.

    A. teath　　　　　　B. teeth　　　　　　C. tethe

4. Did you _____ the blue van?

    A. sea　　　　　　B. sae　　　　　　C. see

5. A _____ is a pretty sight.

    A. sonset　　　　　　B. sunsit　　　　　　C. sunset

6. I do not want a big _____ in my yard.

    A. pool　　　　　　B. pull　　　　　　C. poll

7. We rented a red _____.

    A. carr　　　　　　B. car　　　　　　C. care

8. _____ your teeth every day.

    A. Brush　　　　　　B. Bresh　　　　　　C. Brash

9. Will you go _____ the store with us?

    A. two        B. too        C. to

10. David likes to wear _____ boots.

    A. couboy    B. cawboy    C. cowboy

11. The weather is usually _____ in winter.

    A. cull        B. cool       C. coul

12. Have you seen the North _____?

    A. Starr       B. Star       C. Stare

13. _____ your hands before you eat.

    A. Wach      B. Wosh      C. Wash

14. We had _____ dogs.

    A. two        B. too       C. to

# Unit 36 Test
## Part 2

Circle the correct spelling of the word that belongs in the blank.

1. Is your _____ in December?

    A. birthday          B. brithday          C. birtheday

2. The _____ has a lot of animals.

    A. zou               B. zoo               C. zoe

3. Mara's hair is _____ black.

    A. drak              B. dark              C. darke

4. I _____ I had a lot of money.

    A. wesh              B. wiesh             C. wish

5. Ola was stung by a _____.

    A. bee               B. be                C. bea

6. James put up a new _____.

    A. malebox           B. mialbox           C. mailbox

7. Do you learn spelling at _____?

    A. scool             B. school            C. sckool

8. I have a bruise on my left _____.

    A. arme              B. aerm              C. arm

9. Did you catch a _____?

    A. fishe          B. fich          C. fish

10. _____ house is blue.

    A. Their          B. They're          C. There

11. Dustin likes to look at _____ in the mirror.

    A. himself          B. hemsilf         C. hemself

12. _____ you want to go to the park?

    A. Due          B. Do          C. Doe

# Unit 36 Test
## Part 3

Circle the correct spelling of the word that belongs in the blank.

1. How _____ is it to Donna's house?

   A. fir             B. fare            C. far

2. Wendy lost a _____.

   A. tuth            B. tooth           C. toeth

3. Did you wash your hands _____?

   A. to              B. two             C. too

4. Was Benjamin _____?

   A. outside         B. owtside         C. outsid

5. Where is the other pink _____?

   A. bout            B. boot            C. bute

6. The jeans were _____.

   A. torn            B. tron            C. torne

7. The _____ was after the third number.

   A. desh            B. dash            C. dach

8. _____ going to be tired if they stay up late.

   A. Their           B. There           C. They're

9. Many people do not want to ride on an _____.

    A. airplain          B. airplane          C. areplane

10. Did the parade start at _____?

    A. noon          B. nune          C. nuun

11. I blew the _____ because the car was about to hit my van.

    A. hern          B. hoorn          C. horn

12. God made a _____ through the Red Sea.

    A. path          B. peth          C. paeth

# Unit 36 Test
## Part 4

Circle the correct spelling of the word that belongs in the blank.

1. You should keep your _____ clean.

    A. room          B. roem          C. rume

2. Would you go to the store _____ me?

    A. fore          B. for           C. four

3. _____ of them were Frankie's sisters.

    A. Boath         B. Both          C. Bothe

4. He was sitting right _____.

    A. their         B. they're       C. there

5. Missie _____ called me.

    A. herself       B. hirself       C. hurself

6. Jesus may come _____.

    A. sune          B. soon          C. suun

7. Will you sit down, _____ will you stand?

    A. ore           B. oar           C. or

8. Please go _____ me.

    A. withe         B. weth          C. with

9. The Rea _____ parted for the people to walk through.

    A. Sea          B. See          C. Cea

10. I _____ like to eat peanut butter.

    A. miself          B. myself          C. mysalf

11. You should _____ kind to others.

    A. bee          B. bea          C. be

12. My _____ has pink carpet.

    A. bedroom          B. bidroom          C. bedrume

Answer key
Unit 1

Page 4

A.  1. flat        2. that

B.  1. clap        2. slap

C.  1. brag        2. drag        3. flag

D.  1. match       2. mash

E.  1. fast

F.  1. flat        2. flag

---

Page 5

A.  1. drag     2. flag     3. match    4. brag     5. mash

B.  1. clap     2. fast     3. flat     4. slap     5. that

---

Page 6

| 1. slap | 2. mash | 3. flag | 4. drag | 5. flat |
| 6. clap | 7. fast | 8. brag | 9. match | 10. that |

# Unit 2

Page 10
A.  1. shed  2. bled  3. fled

B. 1. press  2. less  3. mess

C. dwell

D. left

E. step

F. crest

---

Page 11
A.  1. dwell  2. shed  3. left  4. less  5. crest

B.  1. bled  2. fled  3. mess`  4. press  5. step

---

Page 12

1. fled  2. Press  3. mess  4. dwell  5. crest
6. less  7. left  8. shed  9. bled  10. step

251

Unit 3

Page 16
A. 1. brim  2. skim  3. swim

B. 1. chin  2. thin

C. 1. blimp  2. limp

D. 1. wind  2. friend

E. disk

F. friend

---

Page 17
A. 1. blimp  2. thin  3. swim  4. disk
   5. limp  6. skim

B. 1. brim  2. chin  3. friend  4. wind

---

Page 18

1. blimp  2. thin  3. chin  4. swim  5. friend
6. skim  7. disk  8. wind  9. limp  10. brim

# Unit 4

Page 22

A. 1. blot  2. clot  3. spot

B. 1. shop  2. chop  3. crop

C. 1. boss  2. floss

D. 1. cost  2. lost

E. 1. shop  2. chop

---

Page 23

A. 1. shop  2. cost  3. crop  4. floss  5. blot
6. chop  7. lost  8. boss  9. spot  10. clot

---

Page 24

1. boss  2. crop  3. floss  4. lost  5. cost
6. chop  7. blot (or spot)  8. shop  9. spot (or blot)
10. clot

253

Unit 5

Page 28
A. 1. rust    2. must    3. dust

B. 1. brush   2. crush   3. hush

C. plug

D. 1. fuss

E. 1. club    2. buck

---

Page 29
A. 1. club    2. hush    3. must    4. plug    5. rust

B. 1. buck    2. brush   3. dust    4. crush   5. fuss

---

Page 30

1. hush    2. fuss    3. plug    4. crush   5. rust
6. dust    7. club    8. brush   9. must    10. buck

254

# Spelling Review 6- 2nd grade
## (answers)

| Part 1 | Part 2 | Part 3 | Part 4 |
|--------|--------|--------|--------|
| 1. B   | 1. C   | 1. A   | 1. B   |
| 2. A   | 2. A   | 2. B   | 2. A   |
| 3. B   | 3. C   | 3. B   | 3. C   |
| 4. C   | 4. B   | 4. A   | 4. C   |
| 5. C   | 5. B   | 5. C   | 5. B   |
| 6. A   | 6. A   | 6. C   | 6. A   |
| 7. B   | 7. C   | 7. B   | 7. B   |
| 8. C   | 8. B   | 8. A   | 8. C   |
| 9. A   | 9. A   | 9. C   | 9. A   |
| 10. C  | 10. B  | 10. B  | 10. A  |
| 11. B  | 11. A  | 11. B  | 11. C  |
| 12. A  | 12. C  | 12. C  | 12. B  |
|        |        | 13. A  |        |
|        |        | 14. C  |        |

# Unit 7

Page 35
A. 1. take      2. make

B. 1. came      2. name      3. game

C. 1. ate      2. gate

D. 1. m**a**de      2. s**a**fe      3. g**a**ve

E. 1. gave    2. game     3. gate

---

Page 36
A. 1. gave      2. take      3. ate      4. made

B. 1. came      2. game      3. gate
    4. make      5. name      6. safe

C. 1. made      2. came

---

Page 37

| | | | |
|---|---|---|---|
| 1. game | 2. make | 3. name | 4. Take |
| 5. safe | 6. came | 7. gave | 8. ate |
| 9. made | 10. gate | | |

256

# Unit 8

Page 41
A. 1. seed   2. feed   3. need   4. weed
   5. keep   6. peep

B. 1. read   2. beam   3. team   4. seam

C. 1. seed   2. seam

D. peep

E. 1. seed   2. weed

Page 42
A. 1. feed   2. keep   3. read   4. team   5. seam

B. 1. beam   2. need   3. peep
   4. seed   5. weed

C. peep

Page 43
1. seed   2. weed   3. read   4. feed   5. need
6. keep   7. beam   8. peep   9. seam   10. team

257

# Unit 9

**Page 47**
A. 1. ride      2. hide      3. side

B. Child should circle the "v" in five.  Child should circle the "n" in fine.

C. 1. ice      2. nice

D. 1. like      2. time      3. mile

E. five      F. ice

---

**Page 48**
A. 1. like      2. mile      3. nice
    4. ride      5. side      6. time

B. 1. time      2. five      3. hide
    4. fine      5. ice

---

**Page 49**
1. five      2. ice      3. nice      4. like      5. mile
6. time      7. fine      8. ride      9. side      10. Hide

## Unit 10

**Page 53**

A. 1. low          2. bow          3. sow

B. 1. toe          2. hoe          3. doe

C. 1. rode         2. note         3. hole         4. joke

D. 1. hoe          2. hole

E. toe

---

**Page 54**

A. 1. doe          2. low          3. toe
   4. joke         5. note         6. hoe

B. 1. bow          2. hoe          3. hole
   4. rode         5. sow

---

**Page 55**

1. hoe        2. hole  sow        3. toe  doe        4. bow
5. low        6. note  joke       7. rode

## Unit 11

Page 59
A. 1. sold    2. gold    3. cold    4. told    5. old

B. 1. know    2. mow    3. row    4. blow    5. snow


C. 1. told    2. sold

Page 60
A. 1. told    2. sold    3. gold
   4. snow    5. blow    6. cold


B. 1. know    3. old
   2. mow    4. row

C. know


Page 61

A. 1. know    2. cold    3. snow    4. mow
   5. row    6. blow    7. old

B. 1. told    2. sold    3. gold

## Spelling Review 12- 2nd grade
### (answers)

| Part 1 | Part 2 | Part 3 | Part 4 |
|--------|--------|--------|--------|
| 1. B   | 1. A   | 1. A   | 1. A   |
| 2. A   | 2. B   | 2. C   | 2. B   |
| 3. B   | 3. C   | 3. B   | 3. C   |
| 4. C   | 4. C   | 4. B   | 4. C   |
| 5. A   | 5. A   | 5. A   | 5. B   |
| 6. C   | 6. B   | 6. C   | 6. A   |
| 7. B   | 7. A   | 7. C   | 7. C   |
| 8. C   | 8. A   | 8. B   | 8. A   |
| 9. B   | 9. B   | 9. C   | 9. B   |
| 10. A  | 10. A  | 10. A  | 10. B  |
| 11. B  | 11. C  | 11. A  | 11. A  |
| 12. C  | 12. B  | 12. B  | 12. C  |
|        |        |        | 13. C  |
|        |        |        | 14. A  |

# Unit 13

Page 66
A. 1. now      2. how      3. bow      4. cow

B. 1. blew     2. few      3. grew     4. new     5. chew

C. 1. how-cow      2. bow-now      3. blew-few

D. down

---

Page 67
A. 1. new      2. now      3. bow
   4. blew     5. grew     6. cow

B. 1. o    2. o    3. ow
   4. e    5. e    6. e

---

Page 68

A. 1. new           2. chew        3. few         4. how
   5. blew  grew    6. down  cow   7. bow         8. now

## Unit 14

Page 72
A. 1. day     2. way     3. say     4. may    5. pay

B. 1. lake     2. rake     3. wake     4. shake

C. 1. ay     2. a e     3. ay     4. ay
    5. a e     6. a e

---

Page 73
A. 1. say     2. lake     3. day
    4. bake     5. rake

B. 1. may     2. pay     3. shake
    4. wake     5. way

---

Page 74

A. 1. day     2. wake     3. lake     4. May
    5. say     6. bake     7. way     8. pay
    9. rake     10. shake

## Unit 15

Page 78
A. 1. sing 2. ring 3. king 4. wing
   5. thing

B. 1. fill 2. will 3. hill 4. bill 5. mill

C. 1. sing

D. 1. wing 2. will

---

Page 79
A. 1. mill 2. ring 3. thing 4. will

B. 1. bill 2. hill 3. king 4. sing
   5. wing 6. fill

---

Page 80

A. 1. ring 2. sing 3. Fill 4. Will
   5. wing 6. hill 7. mill 8. king
   9. thing 10. bill

## Unit 16

Page 84

A. 1. hand        2. land        3. sand        4. and        5. stand

B. 1. bent        2. went        3. sent        4. tent        5. rent

C. 1. tents       2. lands

D. 1. sent        2. sand        3. stand

---

Page 85

A. 1. and         2. bent        3. sent        4. tent        5. went

B. 1. hand        2. land

C. 1. rent        2. sand        3. stand

---

Page 86

A. 1. hand        2. sand        3. tent        4. bent
   5. and         6. stand       7. rent        8. land
   9. went        10. sent

## Unit 17

Page 90

A. 1. call    2. ball    3. tall    4. fall    5. all

B. 1. well    2. bell    3. fell    4. sell    5. yell

C. 1. ball    2. bell

D. 1. ball    2. well

---

Page 91

A. 1. well    2. sell    3. bell    4. tall    5. yell
     6. ball    7. all    8. fell    9. fall    10. call

---

Page 92

A. 1. ball    2. all    3. bell    4. well
     5. Call    6. tall    7. rent    8. fell
     9. yell    10. fall

Spelling Review 18- 2nd grade
(answers)

| Part 1 | Part 2 | Part 3 | Part 4 |
|--------|--------|--------|--------|
| 1. A   | 1. C   | 1. B   | 1. C   |
| 2. C   | 2. A   | 2. C   | 2. A   |
| 3. B   | 3. B   | 3. B   | 3. B   |
| 4. C   | 4. C   | 4. A   | 4. B   |
| 5. B   | 5. C   | 5. A   | 5. C   |
| 6. A   | 6. A   | 6. C   | 6. A   |
| 7. B   | 7. B   | 7. B   | 7. C   |
| 8. C   | 8. B   | 8. C   | 8. B   |
| 9. A   | 9. A   | 9. A   | 9. A   |
| 10. A  | 10. C  | 10. B  | 10. B  |
| 11. C  | 11. B  | 11. A  | 11. C  |
| 12. A  | 12. A  | 12. C  | 12. A  |
| 13. B  |        |        |        |
| 14. B  |        |        |        |

# Unit 19

Page 97

A. 1. sled    2. slip    3. slide    4. sleep    5. slow

B. 1. plate    2. place    3. plan    4. plane    5. plus

C. 1. sl    2. pl    3. sl    4. pl

---

Page 98

A. 1. sleep    2. sled    3. slip

B. 1. plane    2. plate    3. sled    4. plus
    5. plan    6. slow    7. place    8. slide

---

Page 99

A. 1. plus    2. slide    3. plate    4. slip
    5. Place    6. sled    7. sleep    8. plane
    9. slow    10. plan

Unit 20

Page 103

A. 1. truck     2. try      3. tree     4. trip     5. true

B. 1. bring    2. brown    3. brave    4. broke    5. brick

C. 1. bravely  2. trying

D. 1. trips    2. bricks

---

Page 104

A. 1. brown    2. broke    3. try      4. truck    5. bring

B. 1. tree     2. brave    3. true     4. trip     5. brick

---

Page 105

A. 1. brave    2. try      3. tree     4. brick    5. truck
   6. trip     7. bring    8. brown

B. 1. broke    2. true

269

# Unit 21

Page 109

A. 1. free     2. frog     3. from     4. front     5. friend

B. 1. green    2. grin     3. grass    4. grow      5. gray

C. 1. green    2. grass    3. free

D. 1. green    2. gray

Page 110

A. 1. free     2. friend   3. frog     4. from      5. front

   6. grass    7. gray     8. green    9. grin      10. grow

B. 1. green    2. frog     3. front    4. grin

Page 111

1. frog    2. front    3. friend   4. grass    5. from
6. grin    7. green    8. gray     9. free     10. grow

270

## Unit 22

Page 115

A. 1. sheep  2. shell  3. shine  4. shape
   5. shore  6. shade

B. 1. shop

C. 1. show

D. 1. shoe  2. sheep  3. ship

Page 116

A. 1. shoe  2. sheep  3. shore  4. show  5. shop
   6. shade

B. 1. shape  2. shine  3. shell

C. ship

Page 117

A. 1. shine  2. ship  3. shape  4. shore  5. shoe
   6. show  7. shade  8. sheep  9. shell  10. shop

B. 1. broke  2. true

271

Unit 23

Page 121

A. 1. think  2. thing  3. theft  4. thud  5. thorn

B. 1. tenth  2. math`  3. with  4. Seth  5. bath

C. 1. math  2. bath

D. Seth

---

Page 122

A. 1. bath  2. thorn  3. with  4. tenth

B. 1. think  2. theft  3. Seth  4. math  5. thud
   6. thing

---

Page 123

A. 1. Math  think  2. thorn  tenth  3. bath  4. Seth
   5. thud

B. 1. thing  2. with  3. theft

# Spelling Review 24 - 2nd grade
## (answers)

| Part 1 | Part 2 | Part 3 | Part 4 |
|--------|--------|--------|--------|
| 1. C   | 1. B   | 1. A   | 1. A   |
| 2. A   | 2. A   | 2. C   | 2. A   |
| 3. B   | 3. C   | 3. B   | 3. B   |
| 4. B   | 4. A   | 4. A   | 4. C   |
| 5. C   | 5. B   | 5. B   | 5. A   |
| 6. C   | 6. C   | 6. B   | 6. C   |
| 7. A   | 7. B   | 7. A   | 7. B   |
| 8. B   | 8. B   | 8. C   | 8. C   |
| 9. A   | 9. A   | 9. A   | 9. A   |
| 10. B  | 10. C  | 10. C  | 10. A  |
| 11. C  | 11. A  | 11. C  | 11. C  |
| 12. A  | 12. C  | 12. B  | 12. B  |
|        |        | 13. A  |        |
|        |        | 14. B  |        |

Unit 25

Page 128

A. 1. going     2. looking     3. washing     4. wanting
    5. doing     6. wishing     7. falling     8. blowing
    9. walking     10. growing

B. 1. falling     2. looking

C. 1. growing     2. blowing

---

Page 129

A. 1. blowing     2. doing     3. falling     4. going     5. growing
    6. walking     7. wanting     8. wishing

B. 1. washing     2. looking     3. growing     4. falling

---

Page 130

A. 1. blowing     2. going     3. looking     4. falling     5. wanting
    6. wishing     7. walking     8. washing     9. doing     10. growing

# Unit 26

Page 134

A. 1. birds 2. boys 3. books
   4. ants 5. trees

B. 1. cats 2. birds 3. pets 4. dogs
   5. ants 6. bugs

C. 1. boys 2. girls

D. 1. trees 2. books

E. 1. girls 2. birds

---

Page 135

A. 1. pets 2. girls 3. books 4. trees

B. 1. ants 2. birds 3. books 4. boys
   5. bugs 6. cats 7. dogs

---

Page 136

A. 1. boys  girls 2. birds 3. cats
   4. trees 5. books 6. ants
   7. bugs 8. dogs 9. pets

Unit 27

Page 140

A. 1. sees   2. makes   3. rides
   4. plays  5. rakes   6. jumps

B. 1. looks  2. sleeps  3. sees

C. walks

D. runs

---

Page 141
A. 1. jumps  2. sees   3. sleeps  4. rakes

B. 1. looks  2. makes  3. plays
   4. rides  5. runs   6. walks

---

Page 142

A. 1. sleeps  2. rides  3. makes  4. walks  5. rakes
   6. sees    7. looks  8. jumps  9. plays  10. runs

Unit 28

Page 146

A. 1. snowed  2. played  3. jumped
   4. walked  5. helped  6. wished

B. 1. looked  2. called

C. 1. wished  2. showed  3. brushed

---

Page 147

A. 1. looked  2. played  3. showed  4. wished

B. 1. brushed  2. called  3. helped
   4. jumped   5. snowed  6. walked

---

Page 148

A. 1. snowed  2. looked   3. walked  4. played  5. showed
   6. jumped  7. brushed  8. called  9. wished  10. helped

# Unit 29

Page 152

A. 1. I'm    2. let's    3. he's
   4. can't  5. I'll    6. we're

B. 1. that's  2. he's    3. she's    4. it's

C. 1. don't   2. it's    3. she's

D. 1. can't   2. don't

E. 1. I'm     2. I'll

---

Page 153

A. 1. that's  2. I'll    3. he's    4. I'm     5. let's
   6. can't   7. she's   8. we're   9. don't   10. it's

---

Page 154

A. 1. Let's   2. can't   3. don't   4. It's    5. I'm
   6. That's  7. she's   8. he's    9. We're   10. I'll

Spelling Review 30- 2nd grade
(answers)

| Part 1 | Part 2 | Part 3 | Part 4 |
|--------|--------|--------|--------|
| 1. A   | 1. B   | 1. C   | 1. C   |
| 2. C   | 2. A   | 2. A   | 2. A   |
| 3. C   | 3. C   | 3. B   | 3. B   |
| 4. B   | 4. B   | 4. B   | 4. C   |
| 5. B   | 5. C   | 5. A   | 5. B   |
| 6. A   | 6. A   | 6. C   | 6. A   |
| 7. B   | 7. B   | 7. A   | 7. C   |
| 8. A   | 8. C   | 8. B   | 8. B   |
| 9. C   | 9. A   | 9. C   | 9. C   |
| 10. B  | 10. B  | 10. B  | 10. B  |
| 11. B  | 11. A  | 11. A  | 11. A  |
| 12. C  | 12. C  | 12. B  | 12. A  |
| 13. A  |        |        |        |
| 14. C  |        |        |        |

# Unit 31

**Page 159**

A. 1. zoo      2. do

B. 1. cool      2. pool      3. school

C. 1. soon      2. noon

D. 1. f**oo**d      2. b**oo**t      3. r**oo**m

---

**Page 160**

A. 1. boot      2. zoo      3. soon      4. pool
    5. school      6. noon      7. cool

B. 1. do      2. food      3. room      4. school

---

**Page 161**

A. 1. school      2. zoo      3. pool      4. food
    5. room      6. cool      7. boots      8. do
    9. soon      10. noon

# Unit 32

**Page 165**

A. 1. for  2. or  3. corn  4. torn  5. horn

B. 1. car  2. far  3. dark  4. arm  5. star

C. car

D. corn

E. arm

---

**Page 166**

A. 1. far  2. dark

B. 1. or  2. for

C. 1. torn  2. corn  3. arm
   4. car  5. star  6. horn

---

**Page 167**

A. 1. dark  2. far  3. corn  4. or  5. horn
   6. torn  7. for  8. arm  9. Star  10. car

# Unit 33

Page 171

A. 1. wish    2. fish    3. wash    4. brush    5. dash

B. 1. with    2. path    3. teeth    4. both    5. tooth

C. 1. brush    2. teeth    3. tooth

D. 1. tooth    2. fish

---

Page 172

A. 1. fish    2. tooth    3. both    4. dash    5. with

B. 1. wish    2. path    3. wash    4. teeth    5. brush

---

Page 173

A. 1. fish    2. path    3. Wash    4. both    5. teeth
    6. with    7. Brush    8. Dash    9. tooth    10. Wish

## Unit 34

Page 177

A. 1. be   2. bee   3. two   4. see   5. too

6. to   7. they're   8. their   9. there   10. to

---

Page 178

1. they're   2. too   3. their   4. be   5. there

6. see   7. two   8. sea   9. to   10. bee

---

Page 179

A. 1. bee   2. to   3. There   4. their

5. They're   sea   6. too   7. be   two   8. see

# Unit 35

Page 183

A. 1. birthday  2. airplane  3. sunset  4. outside
   5. cowboy  6. bedroom  7. mailbox  8. herself
   9. myself  10. himself

---

Page 184

A. 1. airplane  2. cowboy  3. sunset  4. birthday
   5. bedroom  6. outside  7. mailbox

B. 1. herself  2. himself  3. myself

---

Page 185

A. 1. birthday  2. sunset  3. herself  4. cowboy
   5. mailbox  6. outside  7. airplane  8. myself
   9. bedroom  10. himself

# Spelling Review 36- 2nd grade
## (answers)

| Part 1 | Part 2 | Part 3 | Part 4 |
|--------|--------|--------|--------|
| 1. B   | 1. A   | 1. C   | 1. A   |
| 2. A   | 2. B   | 2. B   | 2. B   |
| 3. B   | 3. B   | 3. C   | 3. B   |
| 4. C   | 4. C   | 4. A   | 4. C   |
| 5. C   | 5. A   | 5. B   | 5. A   |
| 6. A   | 6. C   | 6. A   | 6. B   |
| 7. B   | 7. B   | 7. B   | 7. C   |
| 8. A   | 8. C   | 8. C   | 8. C   |
| 9. C   | 9. C   | 9. B   | 9. A   |
| 10. C  | 10. A  | 10. A  | 10. B  |
| 11. B  | 11. A  | 11. C  | 11. C  |
| 12. B  | 12. B  | 12. A  | 12. A  |
| 13. C  |        |        |        |
| 14. A  |        |        |        |

www.ingramcontent.com/pod-product-compliance
Lightning Source LLC
Chambersburg PA
CBHW080333170426
43194CB00014B/2543